Streamline

A Business Novel

**Your Path to Government
Efficiency Starts Here**

Richard Baron

Angola Press

Text copyright © 2016 Richard Baron

Published by Angola Press

ISBN: 978-0692717301

Streamline: Your Path to Government Efficiency Starts Here

Copyright © 2016 Richard Baron

Cover design by Jera Publishing

For more information, write to: Success@StreamlineGovt.com

www.StreamlineGovt.com

Published in the United States of America

Publisher's Note: Though the technical and budget situations of government management presented in this story are based on real-life scenarios that have occurred in city and county governments across the United States, all characters and dialogue in this work are entirely fictional. Any resemblance to actual persons or actual government offices is purely coincidental.

Dedication

To Alex and Annie
I do it all for you.
Love, Dad

Acknowledgments

My special thanks goes out to Mary Sojourner, author and writing teacher, for helping me write this book. As a mentor, (www.breakthroughwriting.net) she took me through the painful (for me) process of shifting from a technical writer to a creative writer. I could not have produced this book without her.

I also want to thank my Lean-trained manuscript reviewers for their comments and suggestions. My thanks to Jim Godfrey of Godfrey and Associates, Six Sigma Black Belt David Baron, Carol M. Baron, Esq., Bryan Layton, Assistant County Manager of Navajo County, Arizona, and Jimmy Jayne, County Manager of Navajo County.

Finally, my thanks go to Cindy Wilson and Carol Curtis at the Coconino County Career Center. Cindy and Carol are now my coworkers, but when I was unemployed as a result of the Great Recession, they were there when I needed help from my government. Thank you again, Cindy and Carol.

Introduction

Lean government is my passion.

This book teaches Lean and Six Sigma principles to improve the efficiency of your organization. Efficiency allows your agency to offer more services in a shorter amount of time, with little or no budget increase.

This is a fictional story, based on real-life examples. It is designed to teach you to not only understand the concepts of Lean and Six Sigma, but to equip and empower you to immediately put these skills into practical application.

Consider creating an in-house Streamline team. Assemble a group of employees to read a section of the book and then meet to discuss the concepts. At that meeting, have the team apply those same concepts to an actual problem within your organization. In the end, you will have Lean-educated employees—and a solved problem.

Enjoy your reading, and I look forward to hearing your comments. With the application of Lean Six Sigma tools, we can make government efficient. We have to.

Richard Baron
Lean Six Sigma Black Belt
Process & Project Coordinator
Coconino County, Arizona
Richard@StreamlineGovt.com
www.StreamlineGovt.com

Contents

Part 1

It was a crisp autumn day in the City of Neal, Oregon a farming community in Angola County, the leaves turning magnificent orange, gold, and crimson. A meeting was just breaking up in the historic red brick City Hall. Sam McConnell, the City Manager, watched his colleagues file out. It had been a tough meeting—one of the toughest in Sam McConnell's career. The City Council had walked him through his annual performance review. He had been through these in the past. But he never expected what they had told him this time.

He leaned back in his chair and remembered how the rolling hills, stately trees, and distant snowcapped peaks of the area surrounding Neal had brought him as a young man to the area twenty-two years ago. Fresh from finishing his Master of Public Administration degree in Pennsylvania, he'd taken a job in Community Services for the City of Neal, and had rotated through most of the city departments, the last four years as City Manager. Through all the good and rough times over the years, Sam had never thought that he would go through a meeting like the one he had just had to endure.

He waited for all the others to leave. Council Members Hadley and Wells left together. They were followed by Council Members Brice and Hernandez and Mayor Denim. None of them looked at him or said, "See you later."

Sam looked outside and saw darkness approaching. Looking inside, he felt the room closing in on him. Sam ran his fingers through his thinning hair and thought, *I knew that things were bad, but not this bad.*

Slowly Sam collected his papers and black appointment calendar, and put them carefully into his portfolio. At fifty-seven, Sam had been brought up with computers and electronics, but he preferred the old style printed calendars. They allowed him to see his busy appointment schedule by simply glancing at the open pages wherever he was.

Sam walked from the Council Chambers to his office on the second floor. He studied the plaques and mementos hanging on the wood paneled hallway walls. *We did good work back then,* he thought. *No, we still do good work. I don't care what Trisha says.* He could almost see Trisha Hadley, the City Council Member, smiling at him coolly—in her dress-for-success suit.

Sam found Carl Denley, the Deputy City Manager and his right hand man waiting at his office door. Carl was a bit older than Sam and sliding toward retirement. Sam raised his eyebrows and silently nodded toward his office— not here, come into my office and talk—NOW. They sat down in Sam's office and Sam closed the door.

"How did it go?" Carl asked.

"Not good, I've got ninety days to change things," Sam said.

"Ninety days until what?"

"Until I'm fired."

Carl's eyes widened and his jaw dropped. "I can't believe that. What's the problem?"

"The details don't matter. You already know a lot of it. We've both heard rumblings from the Council in the past, but now things are serious."

Carl leaned forward. "You've got ninety days to change things, or you're let go?"

Sam nodded. "I had a bad feeling when Trisha was elected to the City Council. I knew that she ran her campaign on the promise of improving government, but what can I do, our hands are tied."

"I agree," Carl said. "She has her ideas on how we should run things here, but her ideas don't always jibe with reality—or our funding."

Sam opened the bottom desk drawer, pulled out a bottle of aspirin, and shook a couple pills out. "Care to join me?" Carl waved off the offer. Sam swallowed the pills dry.

Sam leaned back in his chair. "Look Carl, we have got to change something here. I reminded the Council how the population of Neal has increased over the past few years. There are more retirees wanting medical services. More young families with school needs. And more demand for our services. But revenues are flat. Property values are down. Our tax assessments are lower. When the state cut our appropriation that hurt. They basically robbed our money to balance their books. Man, would I like to meet those legislators in a dark alley."

Sam felt his chest tighten. "And *now* the feds cut the road appropriations that we relied on for so long. What the hell are we supposed to do—print money like they do in Washington?"

"Oh, wouldn't that be nice," Carl said.

"Trisha is definitely leading the charge for change," Sam said. "She complained for most of the meeting that her constituents didn't like the services we provide. She talked about the long wait at the dental clinic, the need for more case workers, and the unanswered phone calls to Development Services regarding permits. Let's face it, she has career plans."

Carl sat quiet for a moment. "Did Phil come to your defense at all? I mean he's been on the Council for almost fifteen years. He knows our problems inside and out."

"He tried, but without too much success," Sam said. "He reminded Trisha of the city's growth and all the new services that we need to offer and how the money is just not there."

"And Trisha's response?"

"She heard but didn't acknowledge." Sam lowered his head. "Look Carl, all the Council want me to do is offer more services. Shorten wait times. And improve our customer experience. All with no new money. And I've got ninety days to do this or I'm out of my damn job!"

Sam got out of his chair and started pacing back and forth. "When I got into government work, I thought that it was a noble calling. Helping the little guy always made me the happiest. But back then we had a budget. If you needed to start a new program the money was there. If you needed to repair roads, we received a grant. But those days seem to be over. How can I offer more services to an expanding population when my budgets are flat? What am I supposed to do, pull a rabbit out of a hat?"

Carl sat silently.

Sam stared out his window into the darkness and saw a thin tired man reflected in the glass. "Carl, where are we with regards to city hiring?"

"Over the last several years," Carl said, "our informal policy has been to not hire a replacement when someone left the city. This has certainly put some strain on the current workforce, but it also enabled us to not lay anyone off during these past few years."

There was more silence. *How can we offer more services,* Sam thought, *when we have not been replacing people?*

"Carl, let's take a look at the budget one more time to see what we can do. The bottom line is that we need more bodies. It's that simple. Let's meet first thing tomorrow morning with Jeff from Finance and anyone else who might be able to pull a rabbit out of a hat."

"Will do," Carl said. "Hang in there, pal." He stood and left the office.

Sam lowered his head and thought; *I'm in the fight of my life—for my job.*

Chapter 2

The alarm clock went off in the McConnell's bedroom. Sam opened his eyes and enjoyed a moment of pleasure seeing the early morning light fill the room. Then he remembered—the events of yesterday and what was looming.

He was glad that his wife Laura was already up and making coffee. He needed to be alone to gather his strength—even though she was his best ally. It took every bit of energy Sam had, but he knew that he had to get up and face the day. The smell of the fresh-brewed coffee gave him motivation. He climbed out of bed, pulled on his robe and walked downstairs and into the kitchen.

Laura, a slender woman with soft brown curls, was sitting at the table, eating a croissant, and reading the newspaper. "Hi honey, how'd you sleep?"

"I've had better nights, but your coffee will get me going." Sam walked over to Laura, gave her a kiss on the back of her head and then poured a cup of coffee.

"How is your schedule looking for work today? Full day?" Laura asked.

"I've got a 9 AM meeting and then a few more in the afternoon, but otherwise a normal day."

"I was thinking maybe I could meet you for lunch today," Laura said. "I've got a light day at the real estate office and I have some coverage during lunch."

"Hey, that would be nice," Sam said with a smile. "Where do you want to meet?"

"How about your office around noon?"

"Let's meet away from the office," he said. "I kind of want to get away from that office as much as possible today."

"How about the new Thai restaurant downtown?" Laura asked. "It's about half way between our two offices and we could both walk there."

"Can we meet around 11:30 AM to beat the crowd?"

"I'll be there," Laura said. "I pulled the bread out for you if you want to make some toast. The jelly is already on the table."

"Thanks." Sam made some toast and dug into breakfast. Laura poured herself another cup of coffee. "You seemed a little down last night. Is there anything bothering you?"

Sam made himself look down at his breakfast. "Oh no, just the usual stuff."

After breakfast, Sam showered and dressed. He put on one of his more conservative shirts and ties. He had tried a few times to wear jeans to work, but he felt underdressed—and to tell the truth, a bit too phony. So today he was back to his pleated dress slacks, button down shirt and striped tie.

Sam headed out for the garage and stopped. He knew he needed comfort as the sting from yesterday's meeting with the City Council still hurt—and frightened him. He decided that Laura needed to know sooner, rather than later and walked to the master bedroom where Laura was getting ready for work.

"Did you forget something?" Laura asked.

"No, but I want to tell you about what is going on at work. Come here and sit down with me." They sat at the edge of the bed and Sam held Laura's hand.

"You were right that I was a bit bothered last night, I can never get anything by you. Yesterday I had my annual performance review and well—it didn't go so good."

"What's going on Sam?" Laura said. Her hazel eyes were filled with concern.

"I never thought that I would be saying this, but I may get fired."

Laura stared at him in disbelief. "You what?"

"I may get fired unless I can improve things at work."

"They couldn't do that to you," Laura said. "You have been there for so many years and everyone respects you."

"Everyone maybe except the Council," Sam said.

"You run the city government so well," Laura said. "What's changed?"

"A lot," Sam said. He shrugged. "Maybe I'm not as good as I thought I was—maybe I haven't kept up with the times."

"Honey, you are the best and most professional city manager anyone could hope for."

"I once thought that, but now I'm not so sure."

Laura was quiet for a minute. "I wish I knew more about the situation over there," she said. "This just doesn't seem fair."

Sam laughed. "I wish I didn't know quite so much." He stood and pulled Laura up into a hug. "I appreciate your support, sweetheart. It makes all the difference. How about I see you at 11:30 at that Thai place and I fill you in on more of this mess?"

"OK, honey, I'll see you then." She gave him a tender kiss. "In the meantime, I'll be thinking about you."

* * *

Sam drove to work, grateful for the sun's warmth on a crisp day. The colors on the trees stood in contrast to the sapphire blue sky. It was just the kind of autumn day that Sam loved to be outside. He sighed, pulled into the parking lot, went into his office, started up the computer and logged onto his e-mail account. "Nothing from Trisha or the other Council Members . . . thank god," Sam muttered. He checked his calendar on the computer and sure enough, Carl had set the Finance meeting for 9 AM. He then scanned the many dozens of new e-mails and started working on the ones that needed his immediate attention.

Just before 9 AM, Jeff, the Chief Financial Officer, knocked on Sam's door and walked into Sam's office with his trusty computer tablet in his hand. Jeff was a little younger than Sam or Carl, always a sharp dresser and a real go-getter. *The tablet never seems to leave his hand*, Sam thought. He pictured Jeff someday lying in his coffin with both arms folded over still clutching the tablet to his chest.

Jeff sat down at the oval table. A few seconds later, Carl came in and sat across from Jeff. "Anybody need coffee?" Sam asked and closed his office door. Both men shook their heads no. "Then let's get rolling, gentlemen."

"As you have probably heard by now," Sam said, "the City Council is demanding changes to our services. They have been hearing complaints from their constituents—and, the Council Members are 'the elected'. So by statute, and for their own job security, they have an obligation to pass those problems down to us."

"Was Trisha leading the attack?" Jeff asked. "She is out to make a name for herself and doesn't care if her proposals make sense at all."

"Let's keep the names out of this," Sam said. "I don't want to turn this into a bitch session."

Jeff grinned and nodded.

"They believe," Sam said, "that we are not meeting the needs of our citizens. The council feels that we are not providing the services that our citizens demand and that the services we are offering are below expectations."

"But they know that our employee head count is about 15% less than it was three years ago," Jeff said. "And the city has experienced growth over that time period. How can they—" Sam put up his hand.

"Look, they *can*, it's that simple. Let's not rehash this again and again," Sam said. "No matter what their perception of the situation is, we need to improve what we're doing—and to improve services, we need more people. So I wanted to relook at the budget. As you know, we have not been hiring replacements for anyone that has left the city in over two years."

"Three years," Carl said.

"Maybe the time is right," Sam said, "for us to start adding some more people to help us improve our service offering. Jeff, where are we with regards to the expense budget?"

Jeff looked down at his tablet. "Ah, pretty much right on track. We did get hit when we had to replace some of the equipment in the medical clinic, but we were also helped by a light snow fall this past winter and that saved a bunch on the snow plowing expense."

"What about our employee costs?" Sam asked.

"Right on target as compared with last year," Jeff said. "We haven't had any raises for over two years now and we renegotiated our insurance plan so benefit expenses are right on track."

"Let's talk the revenue side," Sam said. "What are the latest projections?"

"Our revenues are not declining like they have been in previous years," Jeff said. "But they are also not growing. Our sales and property tax are capped per law, so no wiggle room there. The recent growth has increased revenues a bit, but they have been offset by reductions in state and federal funding. As you know, we got the brunt of the shortfall as the state and feds are balancing their budgets by taking away what was promised to us."

Jeff paused and shook his head. "In my opinion . . . we do not have the financial resources to add more employees."

Sam knew that this was the situation. But he wanted to bring it up anyway. He got out of his chair and started pacing around his office.

"Well, our challenge is to offer more and better services while maintaining a flat budget," Sam said. "And unlike private industry, we cannot increase revenue by increasing sales. Our revenue is capped and we must accept that. But to improve services, we need more personnel. What have we done lately for other cost cutting measures?"

"We eliminated the desktop printers," Carl said, "and went to large business hub copiers for most of the departments."

"Yeah, that really helped," Jeff said. "All it did was transfer costs from one department to another. There was no real savings."

"But —" Carl said. Sam put up his hand to halt him.

"What else, Jeff?" Sam asked.

"Well, we are now almost complete with the department reorganization that we started about a year ago," Jeff said. "Unfortunately, we didn't realize any cost reductions though because the reorganization was done to account for the empty positions that we have not been filling over these past years."

"We do run a pretty tight ship with regards to people," Sam said. "And we certainly can't consider getting rid of any employees when we can't keep up with the demand for our services."

"A rock and a hard place," Carl said under his breath.

"What was that?" Sam asked.

"We are stuck between a rock and a hard place," Carl said. "We are severely limited by the revenue that we bring in as most of it is tied to the health of the economy, which we have no control over. And most of our operating expenses are related to personnel costs and we can't consider any layoffs, especially given that we are not meeting the needs of our growing population. So we are stuck between the proverbial rock and a hard place."

The three men were silent as they digested what Carl had said—not that it was a surprise to anyone.

Between a rock and a hard place, Sam thought.

"Jeff, Carl, why don't you get together with your staff and do some thinking. The city has weathered economic storms in the past and we can do it again. However, this time we may need to be a bit creative. Thanks for coming over," Sam said and Jeff and Carl left Sam's office.

* * *

Sam walked from his office down a sunny tree-lined downtown street to meet Laura for lunch. He entered the restaurant and noticed the pungent but delicious smells he associated with Thai food. He saw Laura sitting at a booth and went over to her.

"Hi honey, how are you?" she said.

"Oh OK—just looking forward to spending some time with my lovely wife." He winked and was startled to feel his chest tighten again. Before he could stop himself, he winced.

"Is your chest hurting again?" Laura asked.

"Oh it's OK," Sam said.

"Do you want me to call Dr. Palmer and set an appointment for you?" Laura asked.

"No. No. I'll be fine," Sam said. "It's probably just a little heartburn from tension." Sam knew that Laura knew all too well when he was not being completely honest. Laura reached across the table, embraced Sam's hand, and gave it a loving squeeze. A few seconds later, the waitress appeared and Sam and Laura ordered—Ginger Chicken for Sam, Pad Woon Sen for Laura.

"Sam, tell me more about your day," Laura said.

"I met with Jeff and Carl this morning. We reviewed our actual expenses and projected income. We are pretty much on track, but unfortunately, that means that we don't have the income to hire anyone new."

"What would the new employees do if you could hire them?" Laura asked.

"There are so many vacant positions. We could use more people in just about every department. But that is not an option for us right now. My dilemma is I can't hire more people anytime soon. So I will just need to get my people to work harder, but how?"

"Well Sam, whenever I get stuck, I ask my friends," Laura said. "Why don't you talk with more people at work? You have known them for years and they all respect you."

Sam smiled, "You're right, I will." The waitress set down their drinks and salads and they dug in.

Chapter 3

The next day, Sam took Laura's suggestion to heart and decided to spend part of his morning walking the floors. Although everyone ultimately had to report to him, Sam had developed a close personal bond with many of them. He walked into the Community Services building located a few blocks from City Hall. *When in doubt, ask your friends*, he thought.

Sam swung open the glass door. He heard the clang of three little bells attached by string to the inside door handle. Margaret, the receptionist, looked up from the papers on her desk. "Hi Sam, what brings you here today?"

"I'm here to talk with Gabriela, the department director."

"Oh no problem," Margaret smiled and buzzed the locked door that led to the inner offices. Sam walked in and toward the back.

The new blue and yellow office partitions, together with the many live plants, created a friendly environment in the building. About half of the people in the office were out in the field visiting with seniors or offering health programs at the local schools.

At the back of the large open space were several permanent offices with sheetrock walls and doors. They housed the department director and business manager.

Sam knocked on Gabriela's door. "Hey Sam, how are you?" Gabriela asked and stood up.

"I'm doing fine. I came over to check on my best people," Sam said.

Gabriela grinned. She was a pleasant woman to be around, always smiling, and always ready to crack a joke. "If you are looking for your best people, try next door."

"Gabriela, we go back long enough for me not to take that too seriously," Sam said and took a seat on a well-worn chair in front of Gabriela's desk. "Gabriela, I wanted to see how things are going."

"Busy," Gabriela said. "You know that I'm down three people in my area, and given that there are only fifteen of us, that's a huge hit."

"What happened to those folks?" Sam asked.

"I heard all kinds of reasons; wanting a new challenge, better pay, moving out of the area, nothing really about the city."

"But if you had to put your finger on work reasons, what would they be?" Sam asked.

Gabriela looked down at her desk. Sam waited. When Gabriela didn't speak, Sam said, "Gabriela, off-the-record, what do you think is happening?"

Gabriela looked directly at Sam and said, "Sam, don't take this the wrong way, but a lot of these folks felt too constrained."

"What do you mean?"

"These were good folks, some of my best and brightest," Gabriela said. "But after being here a few years, I heard the rumbling about how things are not changing fast enough. They all wanted to do a good job but felt that by working within our framework, they couldn't accomplish their tasks efficiently enough—and in a timely manner."

"What is your workload like these days?"

"Large and getting larger," Gabriela said. "We do most of our work out in the field visiting seniors, providing lunches, and offering health programs. Over the last several years, we've had quite a demand to help those in need. With three less employees, I can't keep up. Look out there Sam, my people are all busy. We don't have any slackers here."

Sam looked out Gabriela's window and saw a busy office—conversations between co-workers and others preparing for field visits.

"I know that you don't," Sam said. "Look, I know this is hard. We are all working to the max. Keep up the good work." Sam stood and headed for the door.

"Thanks for coming by," Gabriela said.

"Thanks for your willingness to talk."

* * *

Sam left Gabriela's office. Rachael, one of the Community Services staff, greeted him at her cubicle. She wore neatly pressed jeans and a casual blazer as she spent much of her day out in the field.

"Rachael, I've been hearing good things about you," Sam said.

Rachael looked a little surprised. "Thanks. I do enjoy my job."

"Anything we can do to help you?" Sam asked.

"Tell people to stay young and healthy."

Sam laughed. "Not much I can do about that one. What else? What else can we do to motivate you or make your job easier?"

Rachael paused. "Well, there are some policies that we have to follow that seem a bit ridiculous. I mean they have good intention, but they just take so long to do."

"Give me an example," Sam said.

"I'm out in the field two to three times a week and we use a city vehicle. And well, the vehicle check-out process just seems time consuming."

Sam looked at her, but didn't say anything. He wanted her to keep talking, and he could tell it had made her nervous to admit that.

"To check out a vehicle," she said, "we need to write our name on the white board a few days ahead of time. The day we take it out we have to use a form to do an inspection on the vehicle. We look for dents, if the gas is full, if the tires are low. We are even supposed to inspect the wiper blades for damage. You know, like they do at a car rental place. But why are *we* doing this? It is a twenty minute production to fill out that stupid form. I'd rather be visiting the community centers than filling out paperwork."

Sam waited.

"And getting the files ready to go out in the field is a hassle in itself," Rachael said. "We have to find the client records which sometimes are kept in two separate computer databases. Once we find them, I need to print a paper copy so that I can take notes on them. A few months ago I had a small printer on my desk and could make the copies easy. But now IT took away all of the small printers and went to a large copier/printer for the entire office. And the only place they could find to put that big hulking machine was in the back store room."

"So every time I print, I have to walk back there and get the copies. And of course, many times, someone else is printing. Or they are printing on our letterhead. So I wait. And by the time my stuff prints, someone has taken it out of the copier and everything is out of order."

Sam was glad that he was getting Rachael to start opening up about some of the internal problems found in the office.

"I don't want to complain, as I really do like my job," Rachael said. "It just seems like our internal procedures are holding us back from visiting with those in need. And Karen, Steve, and Barb, the three people that left Community Services recently, all felt the same way."

"Rachael thanks for your honesty," Sam said. "The only way for the city to improve is to talk about our problems openly. So thanks again." Sam left Rachael's cubicle.

* * *

Sam walked the few blocks back to his office in City Hall in the old historic part of town. When he walked into the building he saw balloons in the office of the legal department and headed that way. Carol, one of the younger city attorneys smiled at him from her desk.

"Hi Carol, what's the big celebration?" Sam asked.

"This was a welcome back party for me. I was married last week and we just got back from the honeymoon," Carol said.

"Congratulations. I heard that you were getting married. Did everything go OK with the wedding?"

"Oh, it was wonderful. The weather was perfect and I got to see many of my old girlfriends from college."

"Where did you go for the honeymoon?"

"We went to Barbados. Steve and I both love being on a tropical beach."

"I'm glad that you had a good time. Probably lots to catch up on now, huh?"

"Yes, there is," Carol said. "But before I can actually start doing any work, I need to spend my time getting access to my e-mail—*and* entry into the building."

"What do you mean?" Sam said.

"I now have a new last name. Before I got married, I put in the name change form to Human Resources. They updated their records, which automatically shut down the e-mail and my security access code."

"How did that happen?" Sam asked. "Didn't IT get the message that your name changed and set up a new account for you?"

"I guess not. HR said that I needed to go over to IT and fill out another form to get my new e-mail set up."

"What about the building access code?" Sam asked.

"I guess the same thing. Their records show my old last name. So I need to drive over to Facilities later today and fill out another form with my new last name to get a new access code."

Sam didn't like what he was hearing. He shook his head. "I'm sorry you have to go through this."

"One more thing that will take my time is the city issued credit card," Carol said. "I heard from Susan this morning that when a name changes, the old card is automatically shut down. So I need to go over to Finance later this week to get a new card."

"I remember when our IT set up those controls," Sam said. "We instituted the system in the name of efficiency. But unfortunately the efficiency 'gains' we hoped for are being cancelled out by all this extra work. Now you have to spend time getting these necessities of work re-established."

"I guess in the long run we are not being very efficient," Carol said.

"I agree. Anyway, congratulation again on being married. Thank you for your work and your patience."

Carol smiled. "Thanks for stopping by."

* * *

Sam walked upstairs to his office and ate lunch at his desk. *These are good people who just want to do their jobs,* he thought. *But our own policies are getting in the way of getting our work done. It seems like we are holding ourselves back. I guess that that the old saying is true—I have seen the enemy, and they are us.*

Chapter 4

Sam woke and looked at the alarm clock. It was Saturday. He put on his old blue jeans, a well-worn T-shirt, and his favorite work boots. After days of having to make himself crawl out of bed, he couldn't wait to get to work. He was about to indulge in his favorite passion—fixing up old homes.

He went to the kitchen, gulped his coffee and toast and drove out to the house, a former rental property he had purchased a few months ago. He parked in the driveway and studied the house. It was a bungalow built in the 1920's with classic architectural details including bay windows, clapboard siding, and an arched front door. The landscaping had mature trees and the south orientation of the house brought in lots of natural light.

Although the house was in the older part of town, the neighborhood was going through a transformation with younger families buying the affordable homes and fixing them up. This house needed lots of work: an updated kitchen, new paint, and today's project—new windows.

His co-worker, Robert, a younger guy and the head of IT for the City of Neal, pulled up in his red 4 x 4 pick-up truck behind Sam. Robert and Sam had built a strong friendship over the years, after a chance meeting at the local lumberyard. Now they lent each other a hand when needed.

"Howdy Sam," Robert said getting out of his truck.

"Morning and thanks for coming over," Sam said. "Ready to replace some old windows?"

"I sure am," Robert said. "I brought my reciprocating blade. My favorite tool for mass destruction."

They quickly got to work. After a few cuts the old aluminum bedroom window was out. Sam and Robert removed the protective packaging from the new window and got out the screws and caulking.

They replaced three windows before calling in a pizza and soda order. After the food arrived the two took a well-deserved break. As usual, the conversation turned to work.

"I heard you had a pretty tough week," Robert said.

"You know, huh?"

"Everyone seems to know," Robert said. "You know how the office rumor mill works."

"I knew that the Council was not so happy with our performance lately," Sam said. "But I certainly didn't expect that smack-down from Trisha."

"What about running a motivation program to get some extra effort out of the staff?" Robert asked.

"I thought about that as well. I remember the 'employee of the month' awards and the 'employee suggestion' program that the city ran years ago. There was a slight increase in morale and productivity when these programs first came out, but the city eventually stopped the programs."

"As I remember," Robert said, "these programs had a slight positive effect when they first came out, but then after a few months, everything went back to normal. Our 'employee of the month' program seemed more like us preaching to the choir."

"What do you mean?" Sam asked.

"It turned out that the already motivated employees took to the program and wanted recognition. Some of them really stepped up their efforts. The peer pressure between these high performing employees was strong and each wanted bragging rights to win. However, for the vast majority of the employees it really didn't affect them one way or another. So, after about six months, we stopped the program."

"Yeah, I do remember that," Sam said. "Now that I think about it, the 'employee suggestion' program died in a similar way. In fact it even caused some harm to the morale."

"I wasn't here then, what happened?" Robert asked.

"The city asked all employees for suggestions on how to improve things. We got a lot of suggestions all right. But also a lot of finger pointing. People took this as an opportunity to blame the other departments. Or their co-workers. Or their boss for everything that was wrong. No real suggestions on how to fix anything. Only bitching. Others wanted raises and free donuts and coffee, all things we couldn't do. So in the end we stopped the program."

"I can see why," Robert said.

"Most of the ideas were complaints, but very few actually changed the process in any way," Sam said.

Robert glanced away and was silent for a second. "The word 'process' just triggered a thought."

"Well, what is it?" Sam asked.

"Over the years, our software upgrades didn't always give us the results we wanted," Robert said. "For example, we had a process in place with animal control and wanted to buy some software to automate and make things more efficient. We did great research on the products available. Viewed webinars to see the software. And certainly did our up-front work. We would buy the software and overlay it on the existing process. Sometimes things were faster, better, cheaper. You know, all the things you want out of an automated process. But too often we didn't see the results we expected."

"Why's that?" Sam asked.

"After looking at several of what I am calling 'failed upgrades', we realized that we were just automating an inefficient process. We kept the same process we were using and laid software over it. It turns out that automating an inefficient process merely gives you faster inefficiency," Robert said and smiled noting the contradiction of what he said.

"Now," Robert said, "we are now putting a lot of work up-front to Lean out the process, before we apply any software on it."

"What do you mean Lean out?"

"Lean started in the manufacturing world in the 1950's. Now lots of other businesses are seeing the benefit of applying it to their organization. Lean takes the waste out of a process."

"So what gave you the idea to start leaning things out in the IT department?"

"Well I am embarrassed to say, but I kind of backed into it," Robert said.

"How so?"

"I needed help with some of our software upgrades," Robert said. "And I hired a Project Manager, Karen Spencer. She did a lot of project management work in her previous job, so it was a good fit. But what I didn't expect was that Karen brought along with her a lot of experience with *leaning out* processes from her previous manufacturing employers. So we asked her to apply those principles to some of her projects. And the results have been well received so far. The departments that she's worked with seem to really enjoy giving her ideas on how to change the process. These people know the process inside and out. They live it all day long. And with Karen's help they are able design a new process. When we apply the software over this *new* process, the results are very good."

"How exactly does Lean work and will these same Lean techniques work for non-software projects?" Sam asked.

"I sure they would. And best to talk with Karen."

Sam paused. "Do you think this would work at the city?"

"There are now disciplines such as Lean Medical and Lean Financial," Robert said. "So why not Lean Government? Besides, what do you have to lose?"

"My job."

"How about I have Karen meet with you on Monday morning and she can explain in detail how Lean applies to government," Robert said.

"Sounds good. Maybe we can renovate the City of Neal as we are renovating this house," Sam said. "From the inside out."

"I'll set it up," Robert said. "Now let's go finish installing the kitchen window. My son is playing in a little league baseball game this afternoon and I don't want to miss it."

Chapter 5

Karen Spencer was a tall slender woman in her mid-forties, who was finding herself a little nervous as she headed for the meeting with City Manager Sam McConnell. Karen had been with the city for only about nine months and felt very comfortable in her position. And she was curious why Sam wanted to meet with her.

She took the elevator and walked down the hall toward Sam's office. Sam looked up from his desk and smiled warmly. "Karen, thanks for coming over," He said and got up from behind his desk. "Have a seat over at the table."

"I'm delighted to be here," Karen said and took a seat.

"Karen," Sam said, "how are things going for you at the city?"

"Great, I really like the folks that I am working with and hope that I will become an asset for the organization," Karen said. *Jeez, that sounded like I'm interviewing for a job,* Karen thought.

"Don't worry Karen. I hear that you are doing great project management work for our IT department. So keep it up. And I hear that you came from the manufacturing sector where you were involved with improvement initiatives."

"Yes," Karen said. "I came to Neal with my husband a little less than a year ago when his insurance job was transferred here. My background is industrial engineering where we optimize processes. I tried to get a similar job in manufacturing, but as you know, there aren't too many manufacturers here in this rural area."

Sam nodded his head in agreement. "So what brought you to work here?"

"I've done a lot of project management work over the years and was connected with Robert in IT. I interviewed for the job and here I am."

"I'm curious as to your thoughts about how city government compares with some of the private firms you have worked at."

"In the short while that I have been here," Karen said, "I've found that manufacturing and government are essentially very similar. They both offer a product. Manufacturing offers a physical product while government's product is a service. And both a product and service have inputs and outputs and they both rely heavily on a repeatable process."

"Do you find the quality of the people to be any different?" Sam asked.

"Not really," Karen said. "People in government are no better or no worse than those working in private industry with regards to skill level and motivation. We all want to do a good job. If anything, I'd say that the difference is that private industry has competition. And competition spurs on efficiency. Government is and always will be a monopoly. There is no real incentive to make government more efficient outside of public outcries and political promises. The government is such that attempts are made to be more efficient. But its survival is not dependent on it. Government will always be here."

"Yes, I do understand that point," Sam said. "So are you saying that in order to provide more and better services for our citizens, we need to improve our efficiency? How'd you do that with your previous employers?"

"In my previous jobs, I was a process improvement engineer. We were always looking to improve our efficiency, you know, do more with less. And the key was to identify and eliminate waste."

"Do you mean like scrap material?" Sam asked.

"Actually the real waste is found in processes."

"What kind of processes?" Sam asked.

"Everything that an organization does follows a process," Karen said. "To make a product or offer a service, the organization needs to follow certain repeatable steps. When you look at these steps, you'll find lots of activities that don't add any value. This is the waste I am talking about."

"How's that relate to government work?" Sam said. "We don't really produce anything."

"Yes, but we are offering services to our citizens. Whether that is issuing a building permit, or providing medical care, we follow a certain process. Waste can be found in any process."

"Can you give me an example of our waste?" Sam asked.

"Could I suggest that we do a waste walk tomorrow?" Karen said.

"A *what* walk?"

"Simply by walking around your work area, you'll see examples of the eight wastes."

"What do you mean the eight wastes?" Sam asked.

"I'll explain them tomorrow as we find them. Would you like to go?" Karen asked.

"I think I *need* to go on that walk. Let's meet at my office at 9 AM."

"See you then," Karen said and left Sam's office.

Chapter 6

At 9 AM the next day, Karen was at Sam's office. "Come on in," Sam said and gestured for her to take a seat at the oval conference table. "Our talk yesterday spurred me on to do some research on process improvement in government. I found that a lot of government agencies—from the Federal government to small cities—are using this approach. And the results seem to be positive."

"I'm glad you did the research," Karen said. "I have a lot of faith in Lean process improvement."

"Some of the articles stated that Lean process improvement allows government agencies to increase productivity thirty to forty percent—and in some cases even more. I'm starting to see that Lean can increase and improve the services we offer without an increase in the budget. So is Lean process improvement all about making things faster and more cost effective?"

"Somewhat," Karen said. "Lean is more about finding and eliminating waste rather than speeding up a 'Value Added' process."

"What do you mean 'Value Added' process?" Sam asked.

"You can break down any process into discrete steps and each step can then be classified as a 'Value Added' step, a 'Waste' step, or a 'Required' step."

"Can you give me an example that I can relate to," Sam asked.

Karen paused and glanced upwards. "OK, for example, in the morning, we all have our routine for eating breakfast. Let's say that your routine is to make toast with butter and drink a cup of coffee."

"That's close, but I prefer jelly on my toast," Sam said.

"Then jelly it is," Karen said. "Let me draw out an overhead view of an imaginary kitchen on the white board so we can track your movements. This is called a 'Spaghetti Diagram' and it tracks your movement throughout a process. Here is the layout of our imaginary kitchen."

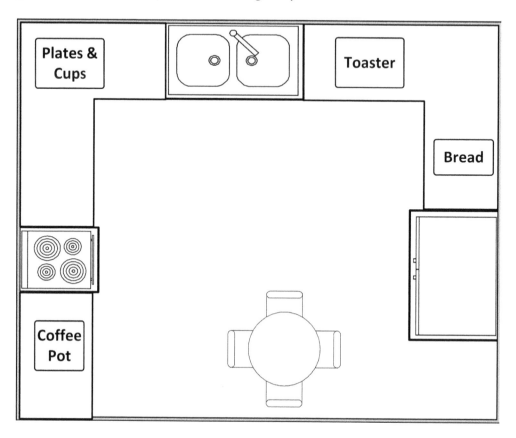

"Let's track the movement of you Sam, our imaginary cook, to see how efficient you are," Karen said. She drew a line on the board to represent the movement of each step.

1. You walk over to the counter that has the coffee pot. Then you reach up and pull out the coffee.

2. You walk over to the sink and fill the pot with water.

3. Then walk back over and turn on the coffee pot.

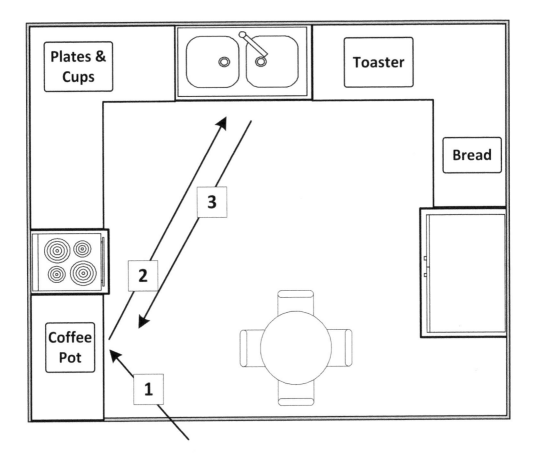

4. Then you walk over to the other counter for bread and get two slices.

5. You then walk over to the toaster and put the bread in the toaster.

6. Then you walk to the refrigerator for the butter.

"You mean jelly," Sam interrupted.

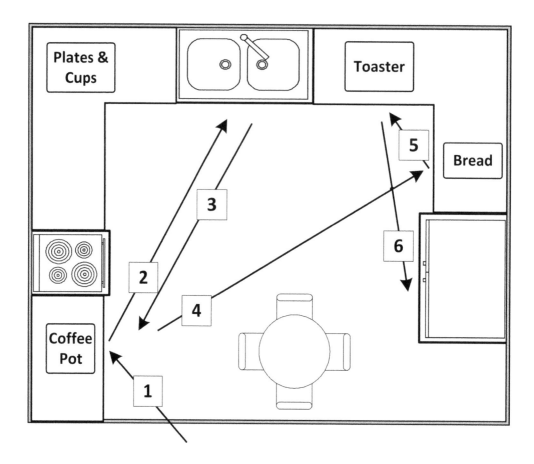

Karen laughed. "Sorry, I forgot that this was *your* routine. OK, so you get out the jelly.

7. You walk to get a plate.

8. When the toast pops, you walk over to the toaster, pull out the bread, put on the jelly and cut the toast in half.

9. Then you get a coffee cup.

10. You walk over to the coffee pot and you have to wait just a short while for the coffee to finish brewing. Then you pour the coffee.

11. You walk over to the table and start eating and reading the newspaper.

12. Once you finish eating, you put the dirty plate and cup in the sink. And finally you head off for the shower."

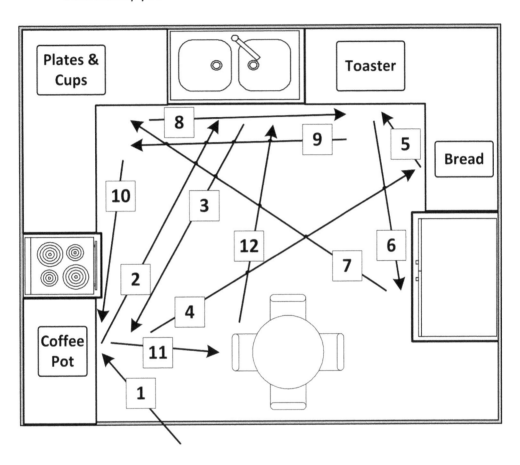

"OK, that sounds close to my routine," Sam said. "So what does this have to do with 'Value Added' steps vs. 'Waste' steps vs. 'Required' steps that you mentioned previously?"

"With all of the above steps for eating breakfast," Karen said, "you can classify each step as a 'Value Added' or 'Waste' or 'Required'. The 'Value Added' steps means that you changed the form or function of the product or service. In the breakfast case, the only steps where the products changed form or function was when you toasted the bread, spread on the jelly, made coffee, and ate and drank. These are the only 'Value Added' steps."

"So what are the other steps?" Sam asked.

"They are 'Waste' steps. They didn't change the form or function of the toast or coffee, they are what some would call 'Non-Value Added' steps."

"But aren't they necessary steps, such as getting out the bread and walking?" Sam asked.

"They may be necessary in your current breakfast routine," Karen said. "But they don't add any value and are therefore classified as waste. These steps should be eliminated or minimized, such as placing the bread above the toaster to eliminate some of the walking. But don't worry; there is an easy way to determine if the step is value added or waste."

"What's that?"

"With each step, ask the question: 'If this step was not done, would it affect the end product that was delivered to the customer?' For example, it we didn't toast the bread and only gave the customer un-toasted bread, would it affect what the customer wanted?"

"Let's see," Sam said. "Since I'm the customer, I wanted toast. Therefore toasting the bread was a 'Value Added' step."

"Exactly," Karen said. "However, if we eliminated the step of *walking* to get the bread, then the end product would remain the same."

"You're right," Sam said. "I'm the customer and I don't care if you walk to get the bread or it's already at the toaster. I only want toasted bread and don't care how you achieve it."

"Right," Karen said. "So walking is a 'Waste' step because if we eliminated this step, we would not change what we provided to the end customer. And it is our job to eliminate or at least minimize the waste steps to be as efficient as possible."

"What about the 'Required' steps?" Sam asked.

"These are steps that don't add any value, but are required given our current constraints."

"For example?" Sam asked.

Karen thought about this question for a moment and said, "For example, keeping the jelly in the refrigerator. Walking over to the refrigerator added no value, but it was 'Required', because we need to keep the jelly cold so it doesn't spoil."

"And since I wanted jelly on my toast, walking to get the jelly was a 'Required' step," Sam said.

"Exactly," Karen said. "You always need to modify the process while considering the customer requirements."

"So let me get this straight," Sam said. "I need to look at the customer requirements, then break down my delivery process into discrete steps and then evaluate if each step is 'Value Added' or 'Waste' or 'Required'?"

"That's correct," Karen said. "And once you've done that, you need to redesign the process to eliminate waste. This is how you'll achieve productivity increases with no or minimal increase in cost."

"Speaking of waste, you mentioned about the eight wastes, tell me more," Sam said.

"Over the years, it has become accepted that there are eight wastes that can be identified in any process," Karen said. "This includes delivering a service as well as making a product. The eight wastes are; Defects, Over Production, Waiting, Non-Utilized People, Transportation, Inventory, Motion, and Extra-Processing."

"Wow, that's a mouthful," Sam said.

"Actually, there's an easy way to remember them. If you say them in the order that I presented, the first letter of each waste spells the word 'downtime'," Karen said and wrote on the whiteboard.

Defects
Over Production
Waiting
Non-Utilized People
Transportation
Inventory
Motion
Extra-Processing

"OK, some of the wastes are self-explanatory," Sam said. "But others aren't. Can you give me an example of each waste?"

"Sure, let's go back to the breakfast example we just talked about," Karen said. "The D stands for defect which is obviously something wrong. In this case, it would mean burning the toast. O or over production is making too much, such as if I made five pieces of toast, but you only wanted two."

"And the other three pieces are waste," Sam said.

"Exactly," Karen said. "The W stands for waiting. Remember how the person had to wait for the coffee to finish brewing? Waiting was a step that added no value. The next waste, N is non-utilized people and is a bit trickier to get a handle on. Think if this person didn't know how to make coffee and had to have someone come over and make it for them. In this case that person was non-utilized, because they were never trained on how to make coffee."

"I understand," Sam said. "It's all about training your people."

Karen nodded her head in agreement.

"T stands for transportation—moving things," Karen said. "In the breakfast case, there was a lot of walking between counters carrying the bread and the empty coffee cup. I is inventory which means having too many of anything. For example, what if this kitchen had twelve loaves of bread in the cabinet? The odds are that some of the bread will get moldy before it can be used and would need to be thrown away."

"And M for motion and E for extra-processing?" Sam asked as he glanced at the words on his white board.

"Motion is a person moving but not carrying anything. In our example the person walked from one side of the kitchen to the other to get bread, jelly, and the dishes. That walking added no value. And finally E is extra processing which is putting too much work into a service or product that the customer doesn't want. For example, our imaginary cook cut the toasted bread in half before they ate it. Maybe the customer didn't want the toast cut in half? So the extra-processing step of cutting the bread in half was a waste."

Sam and Karen were quiet. They both studied the board. "Okay," Sam said, "and the final step is to re-design the process to eliminate the waste steps?"

"Yes it is," Karen said. "In our home kitchens, efficiency is probably not the most important priority for us. But if that kitchen was in a downtown Diner, then efficiency would be important, so more customers could be served in a shorter amount of time."

"What would you do for our fictitious kitchen if it was in one of the mom-and-pop Diners downtown?"

"We'd start by storing the coffee, coffee maker, bread, and toaster close together to eliminate Motion and Transportation," Karen said. "We'd set the toaster to a medium setting so we don't have the Defect of burnt toast. We'd only make as much toast as was ordered to eliminate Overproduction. We would not cut the toast in half unless the customer asked us to, thus eliminating Extra-Processing. We would time the operation so that the server was not Waiting for the coffee to brew. We would only have on hand enough Inventory so that the food didn't spoil, and finally we'd make sure that the server was well trained in how to make coffee and toast so that we didn't have Non-utilized people."

"You certainly see that kind of efficiency in the fast-food chains," Sam said.

"Yes, the food service industry has whole-heartedly embraced the idea of process improvement," Karen said.

Sam smiled. "I get it now. And I believe all of this could work here for the City. How about that Waste Walk."

"Let's go find some waste," Karen said and stood up.

Chapter 7

Sam and Karen made their way downstairs into the Finance office. People were in their cubicles talking on the phone or working at their computers.

"What do you see?" Sam asked.

"Give me a moment to study how the office operates," Karen said. She looked at the office and the neatly arranged cubicles. After a few moments, she noticed a fair amount of people leaving their desks and walking to a back room.

"Let's go look at what's in the back room," Karen said.

The former office had been turned into a storeroom with shelving units filled with office supplies. There was also a large network printer. Every few moments, someone came into the room and pulled their material from the printer and walked back to their desks.

"Do you remember M and T from our talk about the eight wastes?" Karen asked.

"Motion and transportation," Sam said.

"Yes, here is an example of that. Everyone that is printing must leave their desk and walk back to this room to retrieve their material. That's waste of motion as they aren't adding any value when they are walking."

"And the T is transportation of them carrying the material back to their desks," Sam said.

"Exactly," Karen said.

"We recently took out the desktop printers and replaced them with large network printers," Sam said. "Our IT shop said that we would save money going from desktop to network printers. It was all a financial calculation based solely on printing costs."

"But as you can see, that money saved suddenly created a new waste of motion and transportation for all of the city employees," Karen said. "And do you spend more money on printing or employee salaries?"

"Salaries are the main part of the budget," Sam said. "So what we did was optimize one system to the detriment of the other."

"That's what happens when you don't take a holistic view of the *entire* process," Karen said. "I bet that if you *had* mapped out the entire process and assigned costs to both printing and the waste of motion and transportation, your decision might have been different."

Three employees lined up waiting for their material to be printed. They chatted while the machine caught up and left when the network printer kicked-out their material.

"What did you see there?" Karen asked.

"The waste of waiting?" Sam asked.

Karen nodded her head in agreement.

"Let's walk over to the Purchasing office down the hall," Sam said.

* * *

Karen and Sam entered the purchasing office and met with Randy the department head. He was a man in his mid-forties and always wore crazy ties with his normal business suits.

"Nice tie," Sam said. The tie was black, with Jimi Hendrix printed on it.

"Old School," Randy said.

"So, how are things with you this morning?" Sam asked.

"Doing OK," Randy said, "But hey Sam, if you see Carl today let him know that I am waiting for his signature to purchase the tires for Public Works."

"Which order is this?" Sam asked.

"Remember?" Randy said. "We're replacing the tires on several of the city vehicles. The shop foreman signed off on this, as did the Public Works Business Manager, and also Kathy, the Public Works Director."

"Hang on. That order is under our $25,000 limit for authorization. Doesn't Kathy have the authority to buy these?"

"It's well under, but for whatever reason, we need to get Carl's signature as well," Randy said.

"Does Carl ever deny these purchases?" Sam asked.

"Not to my knowledge," Randy said. "Kathy has the final say so, and if Kathy signs off on the purchase, then Carl does as well."

Sam looked at Karen. "This sounds like a waste to me," Sam said.

"It's extra-processing," Karen said. "When you think about it, how many signatures do you need to buy tires? You already have the authorization from the shop foreman, the business manager, and the department director. Carl's signature was merely a rubber stamp as the total order was under $25,000."

"And $25,000 is the maximum level that we authorize our department manager to make on their own accord," Sam said. "Randy, Karen here is helping me recognize all the kinds of waste we have here at the city."

"It sounds like we're requiring a lot of signatures just to buy some tires," Randy said. "What kind of waste did you call this again?"

"Extra-processing," Sam and Karen said simultaneously.

"Wow," Randy said. "I like this waste stuff. Keep me posted."

Sam nodded. "You bet. Karen, let's move on. Let's walk over to the IT office."

Chapter 8

Sam and Karen walked a few blocks down the street to the IT office. This office had once been the city jail. The jail had been moved across town several years ago and this facility sat in disrepair. The IT office wasn't located in the holding cells, but in the office section of the old jail. However, the employees would have told you that the actual prisoners had more room in their cells then they had in their cubicles.

Sam and Karen entered and walked down a corridor to the offices. They passed several rooms filled with equipment—some of the equipment new and some of it old—and came across Marc, an IT technician. "Hi Marc," Sam said. "What's with all of the computers in those side rooms?"

"Some are the new desktop computers that we plan on issuing out over the next several weeks," Marc said. "That was the second room that you passed by. The other two rooms contain all of the old equipment—you know screens, keyboards, old desktops."

"How long has the old stuff been stored there?" Sam asked.

"Some of it may have been sitting there for two to three years," Marc said.

"So why do you keep it?" Karen asked.

"You never know when you may need an old hard drive or motherboard. We figured that since we paid for it originally we might as well get the most use out of it," Marc said.

Just then Chris, Marc's supervisor, walked out of his cubicle. He asked Marc to take a call regarding a computer issue. Marc politely excused himself.

"So Karen, is this an inventory waste?" Sam asked.

"Yes, and it's an inventory of obsolete junk. When you think about it, the equipment was out-of-date when IT replaced it with new equipment. And if this same equipment has been sitting there for two to three years, then it is really obsolete."

"And we have a carrying cost of housing all this material," Sam said. "That alone probably costs us more than the value of the scrap parts."

Sam and Karen continued to walk through the IT offices and came across ten boxes of new computer tablets. Sam picked up one of the boxes. "These are the tablets we purchased for our elections people. They were intended to be used out in the field at the polling places. But I wonder why they are still here; we got them in over a month ago?"

Stacey, a young IT technician, walked by. "Hi Sam," she said.

"Hey Stacey, do you know the story behind these tablets? Why are they still here?" Sam asked.

"RAM storage," Stacey said. "We got these for the elections folks, but someone goofed and didn't order a model with sufficient RAM."

Sam was silent.

"You see," Stacey said, "we loaded the software that the elections department uses on these tablets and there just wasn't enough RAM to run their applications. I mean, the tablets work, but they are real slow. But don't worry, we're sending them back to the vendor and getting models with double the RAM capacity."

"OK, thanks for the update," Sam said.

"No problem," Stacey said and walked down the hall.

"This is the waste of defects," Karen said.

"Someone in IT probably didn't test the elections software prior to ordering the tablets. And that's a defect."

"I understand," Sam said. "We all make mistakes, but now the elections people will be without the tablets for next month's election."

"The truth is," Karen said, "any type of waste lowers our efficiency."

"I'm ready for more," Sam said. "How about we wander over to Public Works?"

* * *

Sam and Karen walked several blocks. "You can see the repair bays here," Sam said as they approached the Public Works facility. Karen nodded. There were big garage bays to repair the pick-up trucks, graders, and snow plows used by the city. They walked into the first bay and were greeted by Phil. He wore grease-stained overalls and safety glasses and held a socket wrench. He pulled off the glasses. "Hey Sam what brings you this way?"

Sam grinned. "Just looking for my missing socket wrench."

Phil shoved the wrench into his pocket. "You can't have mine!"

"Those tires you ordered should be here this week," Sam said. "We need to get one more signature on the purchase order."

"Thanks for the update," Phil said.

"Phil I want you to meet Karen, who is in our IT department."

Phil smiled and reached out his hand for a shake. "Nice to meet you."

"Glad to meet you too," Karen said. "This is quite an impressive place."

"Karen has me on a waste walk," Sam said.

"A waste walk?" Phil said.

"Yes," Karen said, "to find areas where people are wasting time, resources and brain-power."

Phil laughed. "Have I got a thought for you, want to hear it?"

"Sure thing," Sam said.

"Paperwork," Phil said. "I love working on the equipment here in the bay, but I seem to spend half my time filling out paperwork to document what I did. I fill in our log sheet. Then I fill out another form that goes back to the division that operates the equipment. Then another form for finance."

"Why do you do that?" Karen asked.

"That's the way we have always done it around here," Phil said. "Like I mentioned, I don't mind the mechanic work, but do you folks in those fancy air-conditioned offices really need three separate forms filled out every time I turn a wrench?"

"I'll look into it," Sam said. "Anything else that we can help with?"

"I'll think about it and let you know," Phil said.

"Catch you later," Sam said. He and Karen walked on.

"That was the waste of Over-production," Karen said. "We certainly *do* need to keep records of maintenance on the vehicles, but to fill out three *separate* forms all the time? That might be over-kill."

"Yes," Sam said, "that sounds excessive to me too,"

Footsteps pounded behind them. "Oh, one more thing!" Phil yelled out. They waited for Phil to catch-up.

"I did think of something," Phil said. "While you're looking into that paperwork issue, can you also explore having the model number and serial number pre-filled out on the paperwork?"

"What do you mean?" Sam asked.

"When the vehicles get here," Phil said, "someone at the front checks them in, but never fills out the serial number, license plate, mileage info, and other stuff we need. They leave that for us to do. And it takes too much of my time. I would rather be working on the vehicle than recording the license plate info."

"Why don't they do that up front when the vehicle gets here?" Karen asked.

"I guess that they never trained the person to do that. It really is not that hard, but boy would it save me a lot of time in the long run," Phil said.

"Non-utilized people," Karen said looking at Sam. "If we just trained the check-in person to do this task, then the mechanics could spend more time doing their real job."

"I don't care what you call it," Phil said. "Just help me out here, please." He grinned and walked away.

* * *

Sam and Karen walked over to the employee break room. Sam bought two sodas from the vending machine and handed one to Karen. They sat down at a table. "Thanks Sam," Karen said.

"No thank *you*," Sam said. "You taught me a lot today. All of the wastes that you identified were right there plain as day."

"You just need to know what to look for," Karen said.

"So let's see if we saw all eight wastes," Sam said. "D was for the defective IT tablets that the city bought with insufficient memory. O was over-production of Phil filling out three forms. W was the Finance staff waiting for their copies to be printed. And N was the non-utilized front staff here at Public Works who didn't fill in the license plate info."

Karen nodded and said, "T was the un-necessary transportation of the Finance staff carrying their copies back to their desks. I was the inventory of obsolete computers at IT. M was the motion of the Finance staff walking for their copies. And E was the extra-processing of too many signatures to buy some tires."

"I think we got them all," Sam said. "Karen you opened my eyes today. I thought that I knew how the city operates. I thought that we were doing OK. But I can see that there's lots of room for improvement. And it's not with our people as I have always thought. It's with our processes."

They both sat there in silence for a few moments and continued to sip on the sodas. "Thanks again Karen," Sam said. "I need to get back to my office."

"Me too," Karen said.

Chapter 9

Sam returned to his office. Patty, his administrative assistant, waved him down. "You have a visitor in your office," she said.

"Who?" Sam asked.

"Trisha."

Sam had known that sooner or later he would need to speak with Trisha, so today was just as good, or bad, as any other day.

Sam entered his office and saw Council Member Trisha sitting at his oval table. While her stature was on the short side, her forceful personality made up for any lack of height. She was dressed in her usual business suit and had her pad of paper and pen already sitting on the oval table.

"Hi Trisha, how are you?" Sam said. "What brings you here today?"

"I came here today," Trish said, "because I wanted to follow-up on our meeting with the Mayor and other Council Members from last week. What progress have you made?"

"On which area?" Sam asked.

"All of them," Trisha said.

Sam knew that she was irritated.

"Trisha, you know that we have not been able to hire any new people to replace those that have left the city over the past three years," Sam said. "You also know that our revenues are down. And Neal has experienced popula-tion growth. With all of these new people, the demand for services is greater than ever."

"Sam, I don't want excuses," Trisha said. "The citizens of this city elected me because they are not happy with the services they are receiving from the

City of Neal. Almost every day, I get a phone call complaining about the long lines at the medical clinic or the unanswered phone calls to Development Services. Things just have to change. The other Council Members are behind me on this one."

Sam was silent.

"Sam, may I remind you that there are two open Council seats in the upcoming election. Both Lynn and Phil are stepping down as they have reached their term limits. The Mayor and other two Council Members, including me, all believe that changes need to be made."

"I am well aware of the upcoming election," Sam said.

"Good. Then you know that the leading candidates for the two open seats are aligned with us. They want changes. The citizens are demanding it," Trisha said.

"I'm glad that you brought up Development Services a few moments ago," Sam said. "That's the first area I was going to look into for changes."

"What's your plan?" Trisha asked.

"I want to examine the process they use to receive applications and issue building permits," Sam said.

"Good, they certainly need the help."

"I feel real positive that we can make some progress at Development Services," Sam said hoping to wrap up the meeting.

"How does Larry, the department director feel about this?" Trisha asked.

"He should be fine," Sam said and tried to smile. He had not yet talked with Larry.

"OK. Keep me informed of your progress. Sam, you do good work here. Make some improvements so the Council doesn't have to look into a change in leadership."

She stood up and left. Sam sat at the oval table and stared outside. The leaves on the trees had continued with their glorious change of color. It was beautiful, but it also meant that the leaves were all that much closer to falling to the ground. And he had an up-coming performance review. The leaves were an unwelcome reminder of time racing by.

As a city employee, and especially as City Manager, Sam had to remain neutral in politics. Even though his future with the City of Neal was at stake, there was not much that Sam could do but try to eliminate waste, wait and watch the outcome of the election. "The three W's," he muttered.

Sam called Patty. "Patty could you please set up a meeting for me, Larry, and Karen at Development Services tomorrow afternoon?"

"Will do," Patty said.

Chapter 10

Sam and Karen walked over to the Department of Development Services. "Karen," Sam said, "this department is responsible for issuing permits to homeowners and commercial properties when they expand or build new. We've received a lot of complaints recently about poor customer service, long lead times, and contradictory rules."

They entered the front door and walked back to Larry's office. Larry, a chubby man in a blazer, looked up from his computer.

"Larry, let me introduce you to Karen Spencer from the IT Department," Sam said.

"Nice to meet you," Larry said.

"Karen, Larry is the Department Director for Development Services, and has over twenty years of experience in this department."

"I look forward to working with you," Karen said.

Larry laughed. "What do you mean 'working with me'? It's new to me. No offense."

"Larry, I've asked Karen to look at some of your processes here at Development Services," Sam said. "We want help with your backlog."

Larry looked Sam in the eye. "You know what will solve my backlog here Sam, and it's manpower. You know as well as I do that I've had a few people retire or move on. And I'm not being allowed to replace them. We're working as hard as we can. But until I get some more bodies in here, things will not change much."

"I understand Larry," Sam said, "but I want to take a different approach and look at the processes that you use."

"Processes? We did a complete review of them four years ago and made them as efficient as possible," Larry said. "What do you mean you want to look at my processes?"

"Larry, this is something we have to do. We owe it to the citizens of Neal."

Larry stayed silent.

"Larry," Sam said, "would you please get Brad in here now and start reviewing your processes with Karen."

The two men stared at each other for a few seconds.

Karen broke the silence and said, "I would be glad to meet with Brad myself to start the review process."

"All right," Larry said. "I'll give this a try."

Larry walked out of his office and went to Brad's cubicle. He returned to his office with Brad and said, "Brad, this is Karen. I need you to explain the process we use here to issue permits."

"Thank you," Sam said. "Karen, please work with Brad and let me know what you find out. I need to get back to the office to prep for another meeting." Sam walked away.

Chapter 11

"Brad it's nice to meet you," Karen said as she shook Brad's hand. He was an athletic guy and Karen liked his direct gaze and welcoming smile.

"Nice to meet you as well," Brad said. "Why don't we go into this conference room and I can tell you about our permitting process."

"Sounds good," Karen said as the two walked over to the nearby conference room.

Once inside the room, the two sat down and Brad said, "The Department of Development Services is responsible for issuing permits for new construction and renovations. Within our department are three individual divisions; Planning, Safety, and Water Quality."

"So a customer," Karen said, "drops off the permit application with the Department of Development Services and the permit is routed to the three divisions housed here?"

"That's right," Brad said. "But the customer also has to get approval from the Department of Engineering and the Department of Environmental Health. Both of them are located in their own separate buildings."

"So a customer has to drive to three locations in order to get one permit?" Karen asked.

"Yes, that's correct," Brad said. "We've heard a few complaints about that over the years but that's our process."

"So how does the process start?" Karen asked.

"The process starts when a home or business owner requests a permit application. They can either come into the lobby where we give them a paper copy or they can find it on the city's website. It's a four-page document and it contains the information we need to know about their project. The client fills out the form and gives it to the person working the front counter at the Development Services Building. This person starts a new paper file and then accepts a deposit for us to begin work. Here, let me draw the value stream map on the white board for you."

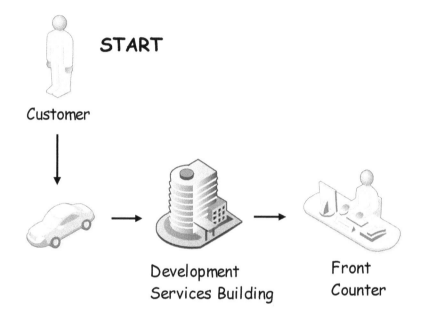

"Oh great," Karen said, "You know about value stream mapping."

"Yep, we mapped all of our process about four years ago," Brad said. "I headed up that project and we tried to make our process as efficient as possible."

"Then continue please," Karen said.

"After the file is opened, we pass it along to the Planning Division. They inspect the file and if anything is missing, they contact the customer. If everything is there, then the review process starts." Brad added to the flow chart on the white board.

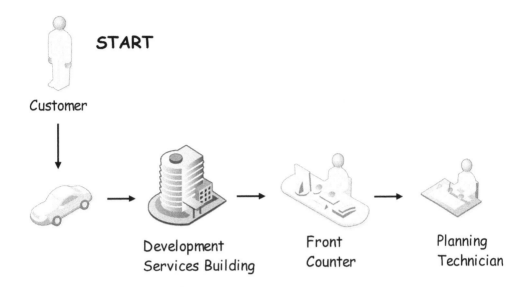

START

Customer

Development
Services Building

Front
Counter

Planning
Technician

"How long does it take between when the file is started and the Planning Department inspects it for completeness?" Karen asked.

"We jump on it right away. Usually within two to three days," Brad said.

"So if a piece of information is missing, it may be two to three days before someone discovers this?" Karen asked. "Could the person at the front counter check to see if the file is complete before sending it on to planning?"

"We thought about that," Brad said, "but the people that work the front counter don't know all of the zoning codes and regulations. Their duty is only to start the file and accept the deposit. Planning then starts their review process by seeing if the property is zoned for what the customer wants to build there. They either give their approval or deny it."

"What happens next?" Karen asked.

"If it is denied, then Planning sends it back to the customer. If it is approved, then the file is sent on to Safety for their review. When Safety gets the file, they look at the application and use the building codes to either accept or deny it. If denied, the file is sent back to the customer. If it is approved, then the file is sent to Water Quality for their review."

"How does the file move from Planning to Safety?" Karen asked.

"It's a paper file," Brad said, "and when one division has finished their work on it, we walk it over to the next division and put it on their desk. You can always tell how far a division is backed up by looking at the stack of applications to be reviewed." Brad added to the existing flow chart on the white board.

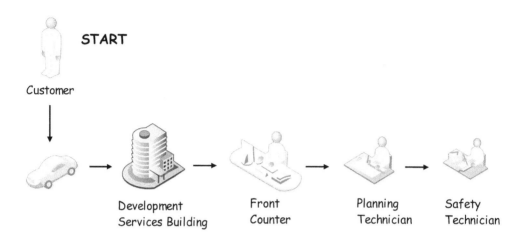

"So following your same pattern," Karen said, "I assume that Water Quality does their review and then either accepts the permit or sends it back to the customer."

"You're right," Brad said.

"So why do you have one division look at the file, make a determination, and then pass it on to the next division?" Karen asked.

"We were working for efficiency," Brad said. "We didn't want any one of our divisions putting too much work into the application only to have it denied by another division. We felt that this was the most efficient way to do that."

"So what percentage of the applications is denied?" Karen asked.

"Over time, almost all permits make it through the process," Brad said. "Sometimes, the customer has to make a few changes. But most applications make it through."

"I would still like to know what exact percentage of the applications is denied." Karen said.

"Probably less than 5%," Brad said.

"I see," Karen said.

Brad added to the flow chart.

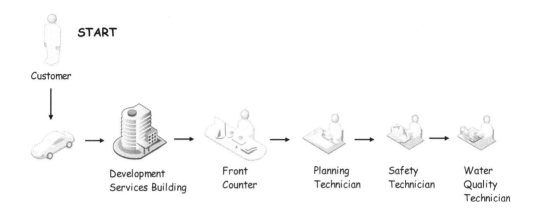

Customer — START

Development Services Building — Front Counter — Planning Technician — Safety Technician — Water Quality Technician

"So once we get to this point our job at Development Services is mostly done," Brad said. "However, the application is not completely through the review process. After the customer has filled out the application at Development Services, they need to drive over to Engineering and Environmental Health and fill out their applications for approval."

"Why a separate application?" Karen asked.

"Engineering is checking to see if the property is in a flood plain. And the Environmental Health Department needs to ensure that they are in compliance with restaurant health regulations, even those applications from homeowners," Brad said.

"Why?" Karen asked.

"That's the way we have always done things here," Brad said. "I heard that in the past one application slipped through and was given approval without Environmental Health having seen it. From then on, Health Department demanded to see *all* applications."

"So here is the flow for Engineering and the Environmental Health Department," Brad said and added to the value stream map on the white board.

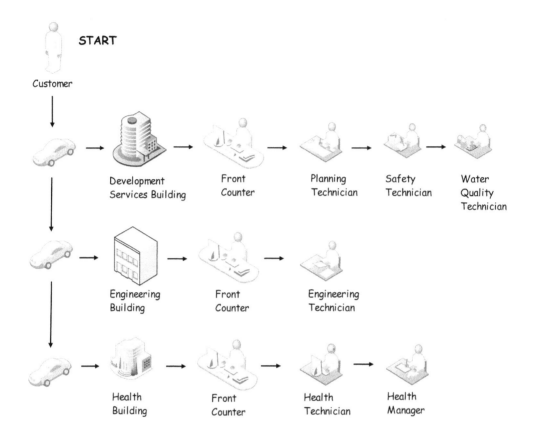

START

Customer

Development Services Building

Front Counter

Planning Technician

Safety Technician

Water Quality Technician

Engineering Building

Front Counter

Engineering Technician

Health Building

Front Counter

Health Technician

Health Manager

"You can see that they are both very similar," Brad said. "We thought that that was the most efficient way."

"Then what happens?" Karen asked.

"We wait for the completed files to be driven over from Engineering and Health and we add them to the file here at Development Services. If all five departments are in agreement, then the permit is issued. If not, then the permit is denied," Brad said and drew on the board.

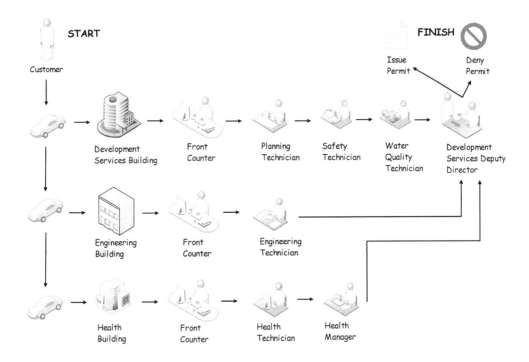

"What's the usual turn-around time from when an application is submitted and the permit is either issued or denied?" Karen asked.

"Given that Engineering is a bit backed up these days," Brad said. "We can usually turn around a permit in about sixty days."

"Two months?" Karen asked.

"That's the best that we can do right now, given our manpower limitations," Brad said.

"That must be frustrating," Karen said.

"It is," Brad said, "but we know that it's the best that we can do."

"Brad I appreciate the time that you have given me," Karen said. "The drawings were very helpful. I need to get back to my office." Karen collected her notes, stood up and walked out of the conference room.

Karen walked back to her office. She shook her head in disbelief. She realized that Development Services did what too many departments do. They optimized the process flow for their *own efficiency* without regard for the customer. However, in the end, they were being very *inefficient* with regards to the customer requirements. *No wonder there have been so many complaints,* she thought. *I will have a lot to report to Sam when I see him tomorrow.*

Chapter 12

Karen arrived at Sam's office the next day eager to talk about her findings.

"Hi Karen, have a seat," Sam said. She sat down at the oval table. Carl walked in.

"Morning Sam," Carl said.

"Karen, I'd like you to meet Carl Denley, the Deputy City Manager," Sam said. "I invited Carl to join us today to learn what you discovered at Development Services."

"Nice to meet you Carl," Karen said.

"You too," Carl said. "I'm curious about what you found—if you don't mind us diving right in."

"No problem," Karen said. "During our meeting, Brad drew a value stream map, which visually depicts the entire process of accepting or denying a permit application. I was a little shocked to learn that the whole process takes almost sixty days to complete."

"I know. We've heard a lot of complaints about this," Carl said.

"Brad told me how Development Services redesigned their process several years back," Karen said. "The problem is that they made the process fit Development Service's requirements and not the customer's requirements. I've seen that all too often, where someone designs an efficient process to satisfy the organization's *internal* needs. However, when you don't consider the customer needs, you miss the mark. It's like getting a strike in bowling, but on the wrong lane."

"What were some of the things you found?" Sam asked. The D-O-W-N-T-I-M-E acronym was still on Sam's white board. Karen walked over to the board.

"Carl, the other day," Sam said, "Karen wrote out the eight wastes on the board. They describe the waste that we may find in our operations."

Karen pointed at the words on the white board and said, "The permit applications are prone for Defects because the city is requiring the customer to fill out three different applications. Anytime that there are three of any-thing—anywhere, anytime—the odds are the three don't match up exactly. It is also Over-production as they should combine the three applications into one. There seems to be a lot of Waiting as the application is routed sequen-tially and not in parallel."

"What do you mean by sequentially?" Sam asked.

"When one department is looking at the file, the other departments are waiting," Karen said. "That's a sequential review. Rather they should do a par-allel review and have all departments review the application at the same time,"

"But what if the application is ultimately denied?" Carl asked. "Isn't that a waste of the other departments reviewing it?"

"I thought of that as well," Karen said. "However, I asked and only about 5% of the applications are denied. So what Development Services did was design their process around the *anomaly* of what only happens 5% of the time. Rather they should have designed it around what happens 95% of the time."

"Go on, please," Sam said.

"There were certainly Non-utilized people at the front counter," Karen said. "These folks could have been easily trained to review the application for completeness. There is a lot of Transportation of carrying the file within Development Services. There was also a lot of Inventory. Brad said you could tell how high the queue was just by looking at the pile of applications sitting on someone's desk. Wasted Motion was also there. People were walking back to their office empty handed after dropping of the file at the next division. And finally, there was Extra-Processing. Each division would contact the customer if there were a problem. There was no one central person doing this job."

"So that's why we take sixty days just to issue a permit," Sam said. Carl nodded.

"Yes, there's a lot of waste that needs to be eliminated," Karen said. "Remember with Lean we are *not* trying to speed up the 'Value Added' pro-cesses such as reviewing the files or red-lining the drawings. Rather we are trying to find and eliminate waste."

"So where do we go from here?" Carl asked. "I mean, Development Services did a complete review of their processes four years ago and this is what we ended up with?"

"The process was theoretically optimized," Karen said. "But they optimized it from Development Service's perspective and didn't consider the customer requirements. For example, why are we asking our customers to drive to three locations and fill out three applications just to get a permit? And I'm sure that sixty days is not an acceptable amount of time from the customer's viewpoint."

"You're right on that point," Sam said. "What do you suggest Karen?"

"I propose that we do a DMAIC analysis of Development Service's processes."

"A what?" Carl said.

"DMAIC is a Six Sigma problem solving methodology," Karen said. "It stands for Define, Measure, Analyze, Improve, and Control."

"And what is Six Sigma?" Sam asked.

"Six Sigma is a business tool for process improvement," Karen said. "It relies heavily on meeting the customer requirements. It also incorporates the many Lean tools such as value stream mapping, Kaizen events, root cause analysis, and other tools to help us analyze the problem. Think of these Lean tools as having a toolbox with a hammer, screwdriver, and wrenches. Every tool is designed for a specific application. With Lean and Six Sigma you use the tool that is most appropriate for the problem that you are trying to solve."

"So tell me again how we would use this, D-M-A-I-C tool?" Sam asked.

"Actually, you pronounce it Da-MA-Ic," Karen said. "The first step is to Define the problem and list the customer requirements. Then you Measure your current process to see if they meet those requirements. Next you Analyze the existing process to find waste. Then you Improve the process. And finally, you set in place Controls so that the new process continues to meet the customer requirements."

"That sounds rather straightforward to me," Carl said.

"It is," Karen said. "DMAIC uses hard facts and is a very organized problem solving method which produces excellent results."

"Will it work at Development Services?" Sam asked.

"DMAIC will work on any process, and yes, it will eliminate waste at Development Services," Karen said.

"Then you have my authorization to go ahead with DMAIC," Sam said. "I'll call Robert your supervisor and let him know that this is now your number one work priority. Carl, I want you to be my lead on this project. Stay in close contact with Karen and support her however she needs. Please also speak with Larry and let him know that Karen has my authorization to use DMAIC to help redesign the process we use at Development Services."

"Will do," Carl said. "I'll keep you informed as to the progress."

"Thank you both for your time," Sam said. "I think we are going to see some powerful changes around here."

"Thank you for being open," Karen said. She and Carl gathered up their things and left Sam's office.

Karen walked back to her office and smiled. She was excited to apply what she knew about Lean and Six Sigma to Development Services. But she was also a little apprehensive. She knew that there was a lot of work ahead of her.

END OF PART 1

* * *

Part 2

Carl walked up to the older house that Sam was renovating and looked in the front bay window. "Hello, anyone here?" The living room was full of tools, lumber, and drop cloths, half way between disrepair and renovation. "Hey, anyone in here?"

Sam walked into the living room. "Hi, Carl what brings you here?"

"I just wanted to see how you were doing," Carl said. "I went to your house and Laura said that you were working on the rental house. I hope you don't mind that I came over on a Saturday."

"No, it's good to see you," Sam said and took off his leather tool belt. "And I could use a break from installing the kitchen cabinet." He pointed to his toolbox. "Here, have a seat. It's the closest thing I have to a chair in this place."

"Hope I fit," Carl said and sat down. "Mind a little shop talk?" Carl said.

"Have at it," Sam said.

"So what are we going to do," Carl said, "now that both of Trisha's candidates were elected?"

"I'm not sure," Sam said. "But Trisha was right that both of the candidates she supported were overwhelmingly elected as the new City Council Members. I've met with them both several weeks ago, but I didn't get a real sense of their priorities."

"Being new," Carl said, "I'm sure that they'll both look to Trisha for her guidance. And we both know all too well that she's not shy when it comes to speaking her mind."

Sam grinned and shook his head. "That's for sure."

"Sam, tell me more about what the Council wanted when you had the performance review last month. Did they give you any specific guidance?"

"No," Sam said. "They just said that the performance of Neal's government is not keeping up with the times. They said the citizens were complaining of slow service and some of the business leaders in town couldn't get permits to expand their operations."

"Trisha certainly bows down to the power brokers in this area," Carl said.

"That's one of the reasons why I asked Karen to look into Development Services," Sam said. "I figure that if we could make some progress there, it would buy us some time. I know that it has only been a few days, but has Karen made any progress?"

"I talked with her on Friday," Carl said, "and she mentioned that she was trying to determine who to put on the DMAIC team. I offered a few suggestions. I think she'll be seeing you on Monday to get your opinion."

"I'll be glad to give her some names of potential team members," Sam said.

"Sam, I do have faith that this Lean improvement effort will pay off," Carl said. "I think that the Council will be pleased by the results and you'll keep your job."

"Thanks, Carl," Sam said.

"Don't worry, I'll definitely keep a close watch on Karen's progress and let you know," Carl said. "Sam, I also have an idea that I wanted to float by you. What if I took the initiative and met with all of the Council Members individually? This would give me a good sense of what their priorities are and maybe I can give you some insight when we meet with them at the next Council meeting."

"That's not a bad idea," Sam said. "It would certainly help to have this information when my performance review comes up in eight weeks."

"Sam, why don't you relax and let me handle this?" Carl said.

"I appreciate it Carl. I know that I can count on you. Come on let me show you around this dump . . . I mean my work in progress."

"Then, maybe a beer and pizza?"

"I'm sold." Sam said.

Chapter 14

Patty stepped into Sam's office on Monday morning. "Sam, Karen's here to see you."

"I'll be right out to get her." He punched in a few more budget numbers on the computer, saved the file and walked out into the waiting area.

Karen looked up and smiled.

"Hi Karen, good to see you," Sam said.

"Thanks for taking the time," Karen said.

Sam led her into his office and pointed to a chair at the big table. "Have a seat at the oval table. Carl told me that you wanted to get my opinions on whom to place on the DMAIC team. Is that right?"

"Yes it is," Karen said. "I've been a DMAIC Project Manager many times before. I know the critical importance of putting the right people on the team. With the wrong people, the entire effort may fail. So I wanted to speak with you and get your opinion."

"Sure, go ahead and I can give you some suggestions," Sam said.

"Great," Karen said. "I want to have about five to seven people on the team. Having a team with more than eight members is a bit tough to manage. And each member needs to have direct experience with the process."

"How about Larry the Department Director?" Sam asked. "He has been there for over twenty years now."

"I've found that department directors aren't always the best to be on the team," Karen said. "They may be personally invested in the status quo and not want to make changes. Also, some directors have a theoretical idea as to how their operation works, but they don't know what is actually done day in and day out. Finally, the department director may be intimidating to the other members and then no one speaks up."

"I get it," Sam said. "The team should be made up of peers so they all feel equally invested in the project."

"What I really need," Karen said, "is representation from each of the five divisions involved: Planning, Safety, Water Quality, Engineering and Environmental Health. And also someone from the Development Services Department who has a good overview of the entire process. These folks should be subject matter experts with real life experience. But most importantly the team members must have a willingness to change. Otherwise they may inadvertently sabotage the team's efforts."

"Let me think about this," Sam said. "Three people that come to mind immediately are Keisha Wilson from Environmental Health, Cindy Heinz from Planning and Tim Dresser from Engineering. Do you know these people?"

"I've worked with Keisha and Tim before," Karen said. "They are creative people who interact well with others. Is Cindy like this as well?"

"Yes, she is," Sam said.

"Great," Karen said. "I'll be in contact with them soon. But what about someone to represent Safety and Water Quality?"

"I would suggest Adam Thatcher from Safety," Sam said. "He would be a good choice. But no one comes to mind from Water Quality."

"When I met with Carl last week," Karen said, "he suggested Patel Sami. Do you know him?"

"I've heard the name," Sam said, "but if Carl recommends him, then I would as well."

"To finish off the team," Karen said, "I was planning on asking Brad Able from the Development Services Department. When I met with him last week, he seemed to have a good overview of the entire process."

"However, Brad helped with the Development Services redesign efforts years ago," Sam said. "Do you think he may be too invested in the existing process?"

"I didn't get that impression when I met with him," Karen said. "He seemed open to new ideas, plus he has experience with value stream mapping."

"OK," Sam said. "Could you please recap the team?"

"I have Keisha Wilson from Environmental Health, Cindy Heinz from Planning, Tim Dresser from Engineering, Patel Sami from Water Quality, and Adam Thatcher from Safety," Karen said. "Brad Able will represent the Development Services Department and I will be the facilitator."

"Sounds like a winning team," Sam said.

"The other thing I'll do," Karen said, "is put together some educational material that I'll pass out during the meeting. I found it best to start the DMAIC effort with some training on Lean, Six Sigma and the eight wastes."

"I was certainly enlightened," Sam said, "when you taught me the eight wastes and we did our waste walk together. When will you get started with the DMAIC project?"

"I'll reach out to these people today," Karen said. "And Carl said that he will speak with their supervisors to give them authorization to work on the project."

"With you and Carl on this project," Sam said, "I feel better already."

Chapter 15

The next morning Karen headed out of her driveway for work and down her tree-lined street. *What a beautiful day,* she thought. *I just love the yellow and red leaves. It's too bad that the colors represent the coming of winter. But I guess it's all part of the rebirth process. It's just like the process redesign at Development Services. In order to create a new process, we need to understand the old, and if necessary eliminate it. Just as the leaves are doing right now.*

She pulled into the Neal City Hall parking lot, went inside, set up the training materials and prepared the conference room for the upcoming meeting.

Adam walked into the conference room. "Good morning Karen."

"Good morning to you too," Karen said. "How are you?"

"Excited to be here," Adam said. "Thanks for including me on the team."

"My pleasure," Karen said. "You came highly recommended."

Cindy and Keisha entered the room together. "Hello everyone," Cindy said.

"Good morning," Keisha said.

"Thanks for coming over," Karen said.

Patel, Brad and Tim walked in. "How is everyone?" Brad asked.

"Glad to be here," Keisha said.

"It looks like we are all here," Brad said.

"Yes and thanks for coming everyone," Karen said. "We have two objectives at today's kick-off meeting. The first is to introduce everyone to the concepts of the Lean, Six Sigma, and process mapping, and the second is to write the problem statement. I think everyone knows everyone here, but first let's go around the table and check in."

"Hi, I'm Brad from Development Services."

"Tim from Engineering."

"Cindy with the Planning Division."

"Keisha with Environmental Health."

"I'm Patel and I'm with Water Quality."

"And I'm Adam with Safety."

"Thanks everyone," Karen said. "Today we'll meet for only about ninety minutes and then we'll meet regularly over the course of the next several weeks. Any questions before we start?"

"What about our day-to-day responsibilities?" Keisha asked.

"Good question," Karen said. "Carl Denley has talked with all of your supervisors to let them know that you have been selected to be a part of this DMAIC team. Each meeting will be relatively short so that you can deal with any pressing issues when you return to your respective offices."

"Darn," Keisha said. "I was hoping we could all go home early when we finished our meeting this morning."

"Sorry," Karen said, "no such luck. So let's start with an introduction to Lean and Six Sigma. Does anyone here have any experience with process improvement?"

Cindy, Brad and Tim raised their hands. "At my last position with the county, we did a process flow mapping project. That was several years ago." Tim said.

"I had some training on Six Sigma, but no actual hands-on project," Cindy said.

"I was involved in the value stream mapping of Development Services several years ago," Brad said.

"Good to know," Karen said. "I may call on you as we move forward. Let's start off by giving an overview of Lean and Six Sigma." She passed out reference material to the team. "In simplest terms, Lean is the identification and elimination of waste. We can find waste in any process. By finding and eliminating waste in a service process, we are able to lower the time and cost to offer the service—and ultimately offer the service to more citizens."

"Six Sigma is a structured business tool for problem solving," Karen said. "It focuses on meeting customer requirements. Six Sigma relies heavily on the use of data for decision-making. At the heart of Six Sigma is DMAIC, pronounced Da-MA-Ic, which is an acronym for Define, Analyze, Measure,

Improve, and Control. By combining Lean principles with Six Sigma methodology, we have a very powerful tool for improving operations."

"Any questions at this point?" Karen asked. The team was silent.

"OK, let's take a deeper dive into Lean," Karen said. "Some key terms that you need to be aware of are process mapping, identifying the eight wastes, and labeling a process step as either 'Value Added', 'Waste', or 'Required'."

Karen turned toward Tim and asked, "You said that you were involved in a process mapping exercise in a previous position?"

"Yes, I was," Tim said. "I was in the facilities division at Angola County and we looked at improving the process flow used for delivering the mail within our building."

"Can you give us an overview of what process mapping is?" Karen asked.

"As I remember," Tim said, "process mapping is a pictorial representation of any process or set of activities. We used rectangular boxes to demonstrate an activity, a diamond shape to represent if there was a decision, and an oval shape to indicate the start and stop of the process, and an arrow to indicate the direction of flow."

Karen drew these symbols on the white board as Tim was speaking.

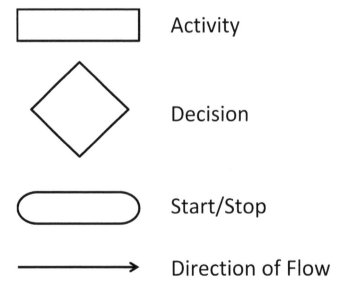

"Did you use swim lanes?" Karen asked.

"Oh yea, I forgot about that," Tim said. "Swim lanes contain all of the activities that occur for a particular person or department. It's kind of like looking down on a swimming pool and seeing people in the individual lanes."

"Could you draw the mail delivery process used at the county for us?" Karen asked.

Tim went up to the white board and started sketching out the process map for delivering mail at Angola County.

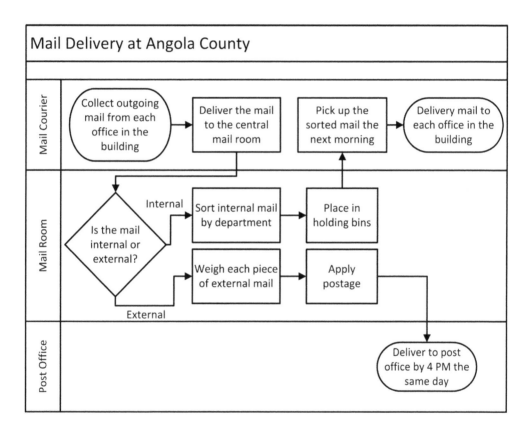

"Delivering internal mail," Tim said, "is a pretty simple process. It only has the three swim lanes of 'mail courier', 'mail room', and 'post office'. You can see the steps above. In addition to the process steps we also estimated times for each operation on a separate page. This gave us an idea as to how long the entire process took. We then determined the true 'processing time' from the 'lead time'."

"I'm so glad that you brought that up," Karen said. "Just to let everyone know, 'lead time' is how long it takes to complete the entire operation from start to stop. It includes all of the steps involved including 'Waste' steps such as waiting. The 'processing time' is how long a 'Value Added' activity occurs at each individual step in the process."

"If I remember right," Tim said, "the 'lead time' to deliver internal mail was about twenty-four hours. Meaning that if someone placed inter-office mail in his or her department out box, we would deliver it to the recipient the next day. However, when we looked at how much time was actually spent *processing* that letter, such as sorting it, the actual 'processing time' was under one hour."

"And what was happening the other twenty-three hours?" Karen asked.

"It was waste," Tim said. "The inter-office letter was just sitting in a bin or in a cart. Nothing was really being done with it."

"Thanks Tim," Karen said. "That's a great explanation of process mapping. Once you map out a process, you want to go back and look at each step to see if it is a 'Value Added' step, 'Waste', or 'Required'. A 'Value Added' step changes the form or function of the item in question; a 'Waste' step adds no value and should be eliminated and a 'Required' step adds no value, but is required and should be minimized. Let's look back at Tim's process map of delivering mail. Steps that are 'Value Added' include sorting internal from external mail and applying postage to the external mail because these steps changed the form or function. In this example, we can see that placing mail in the holding bins and letting them sit overnight didn't add any value. These are 'Waste' steps and should be eliminated."

"A 'Required' step is one that did not add value, but is required given the situation," Karen said. "For our example we weighed the outgoing mail. This did not add any value, but was required in order to apply the correct postage. Does this make sense to everyone?"

"It does," Keisha said. "But you mentioned before about the eight wastes. What do you mean by the eight wastes?"

"People have identified eight wastes that apply to operations," Karen said. "The eight wastes spell out the work D-O-W-N-T-I-M-E."

Karen passed out training material that listed the wastes.

Defects
Over Production
Waiting
Non-Utilized People
Transportation
Inventory
Motion
Extra-Processing

"Let me give a brief definition of each waste," Karen said. "And then I'll ask you to give me an example of that waste in your work life. Sound good?"

"Works for me," Adam said.

"A defect," Karen said, "is something that you thought was complete but needs to be revisited as it didn't meet the customer's requirement. For example, if a customer submitted their permit application at Development Services, but didn't fill out all of the information needed, then this is a defect."

"Isn't that a defect from the customer?" Adam asked.

"It is," Karen said, "but it becomes a defect for *you* if someone doesn't inspect that application form first to find the error. If the person at the counter passes the incomplete form into the system, it becomes a defect for you."

"That makes sense," Keisha said.

"Over Production," Karen said, "is making too much of something."

"I've got an example of that," Tim said. "Last week my supervisor asked me for a 'roads condition' report. So I gave him all of the tables, graphs, and charts, explaining the current state of our roads in the city. I printed it all out in color and gave it to him in a three ring binder. Well, it turns out that all he wanted was a one-page summary listing the miles of roads in 'good', 'fair', and 'poor' condition."

"What you did is over-produce," Karen said. "The lesson learned is that if we don't ask for the customer requirements precisely, we may be doing a lot of over-production. The next waste is waiting, which means that we are waiting for information, or signatures, or even equipment to be operational. Any examples of this?"

Keisha raised her hand. "I'm always waiting for signatures. When I finish my work on a permit application I need to get my supervisor to sign-off on it. Too often that may take one to two days."

"And is that signature even necessary?" Karen asked.

"What do you mean?" Keisha asked.

"Too often," Karen said, "we have these procedures in place that we don't even question. For example, does your supervisor sign every permit application? Or does she ever *question* your work?"

"No," Keisha said. "She goes by what I recommend as I have more technical experience that she has."

"OK, the next waste," Karen said, "is non-utilized people. This is where we don't authorize our own people to make decisions."

"Couldn't we argue," Adam said, "that not authorizing Keisha to make the final determination on the permit application is a non-utilized person waste?"

"That's a very good point," Karen said. "Good job Adam."

"Thanks," Adam said.

"T is for transportation," Karen said. "This is where something is being moved."

"We do a lot of that," Brad said, "with the paper permit application. We always seem to be moving it from one desk to another."

"Any easy way to eliminate this waste?" Karen asked.

"If the file was electronic," Patel said, "that would certainly minimize this waste."

"And we will be looking into that idea in future meetings," Karen said. "OK, we have three more wastes to go through. And they are inventory, motion, and extra-processing. While it's easy to think of the waste of inventory in terms of too many paper clips, the more destructive inventory waste is unbalanced workloads."

"Can you explain that more?" Keisha asked.

"Sure," Karen said. "Let's assume that we have a process that is worked on sequentially by three people, persons A, B, and C. An unbalanced workload means that person A and C can finish their work on an application in five minutes. However, person B needs twenty minutes to do their work. What's going to happen when applications are reviewed by persons A, B, and C?"

"Person A would finish their review in five minutes," Brad said. "And since person B takes twenty minutes to do their work, a bunch of files will be there waiting for person B to work on."

"And what about person C?" Karen asked.

"They would be sitting there with nothing to do," Tim said.

"That's right," Karen said. "This is an example of the waste of inventory, meaning an inventory of files waiting for person B to review. It resulted from an unbalanced workload."

"I see that every day," Brad said, "with our current process at Development Services."

"Next we have motion," Karen said. "The waste of motion can occur even if we are sitting at our desks."

"I can testify to this one," Patel said. "The other day I made some training materials for my staff. Instead of saving it as a Power Point® document as I usually do, I saved it as a Word® file. Boy, I spent twenty minutes the next day trying to find that file because I was looking in my Power Point® documents."

"Good example," Karen said. "Motion can either be unnecessary walking, or clicking on the keyboard, or making phone calls to find something."

"The last of the eight wastes," Karen said, "is extra-processing. Any examples?"

"I've got a great example for that," Brad said.

"What is it?" Karen asked.

"Before I worked at the city," Brad said, "I was at a business where we would enter a customer's information into two or three databases. It seemed like we were extra-processing, because once we entered the info into the computer, it seemed wasteful to re-enter it over and over again."

"Good example Brad," Karen said. "Now let's apply the eight wastes to a real life process that we have all been through many times before, such as going to a doctor's office. Who's been to the doctor lately?"

"I went last week," Patel said.

Tim grinned. "Spare us the details what was wrong with you."

"Don't worry, it was just some arthritis in my knee. I've been seeing this doctor for some time about it."

"OK, can you walk us through the visit?" Karen asked. "Tell us what steps you had to go through, and then as a group we will see if each step was 'Value Added', 'Waste', or 'Required'."

"The appointment was last Tuesday at 10 AM," Patel said. "I went to the front desk and signed in."

"Did they ask to see your insurance card?" Karen asked.

"Yes they did," Patel said. "They photocopied the front and back of it."

"OK, then what?" Karen asked.

"I sat in the waiting room for about ten minutes reading a magazine," Patel said. "Then someone called my name and they walked me to a nurse's station. They weighed me, took my height, took my temperature, and then my blood pressure. After that, they walked me to a room in the back and I sat."

"How long did you wait there?" Karen asked.

Patel laughed. "Long enough that I started reading their pamphlet on hemorrhoids."

"OK then what?" Karen asked.

"After about ten minutes," Patel said, "the doctor's assistant came in and asked some questions about why I was seeing the doctor. Then the assistant left and about three minutes later, my doctor came in. The doctor asked me some of the same questions that the assistant asked me a few minutes earlier. Eventually he looked at my knee and we talked about the medicine he prescribed. We talked for about five minutes and then my doctor increased the dosage on my medicine. I then checked out at the front desk and drove away."

"So how long did the appointment take?" Karen asked.

"About an hour," Patel said.

"So you were at the doctor's office for one hour. That means that the lead time was sixty minutes," Karen said. "OK, everyone look at the eight wastes listed on the white board and see what you can identify from Patel's visit to the doctor?"

The team looked at the page listing D-O-W-N-T-I-M-E. Cindy said, "There's always a lot of waiting when I go to the doctor."

"Me too," Brad said.

"There's also a lot of motion of moving between the waiting room, the nurse's station, and that little back room," Adam said.

"What about the paperwork when you first got to the doctor's office?" Karen asked.

"I always have to fill out a new form with my address, insurance card, and medical condition every time I go to my doctor," Adam said.

"That seems to me like a lot of extra-processing," Cindy said. "Why can't they just ask us if anything has changed since the last time we were there?"

"I agree," Brad said. "And the assistant and the doctor seem to ask you the same questions. That seems like a lot of extra-processing."

"OK, we have just described the 'Waste' steps," Karen said. "These steps did not change form or function, and as consumers we are not willing to pay for these steps."

"So what are the 'Required' steps?" Karen asked.

"I guess seeing the insurance card was required," Brad said, "as well at taking Patel's temperature and blood pressure."

"You're right," Karen said. "These steps didn't change the form or function, but they were required. For example, they need to see the insurance card for billing purposes and they need to check Patel's vitals to help with the diagnosis. They didn't add value, but are required. OK, then what were the 'Value Added' steps?"

The group was silent for a moment. Tim said, "I guess it was the time that Patel spent with the doctor."

"Yes, you're right," Karen said. "Talking with the doctor changed the form or function as Patel received some guidance from the doctor to help with his knee. We as consumers are willing to pay for the information, and we will have to assume that it was done right."

"He's a good doctor, I've been with him for years," Patel said.

"So when we mapped out the process of going to a doctor," Karen said, "we found a lot of 'Waste', some 'Required' steps, and one 'Value Added' step. And that 'Value Added' step only lasted about five minutes. Think about that . . . a doctor's office visit is usually about one hour and yet only about five minutes of it is truly 'Value Added'. So even though the 'lead time' for a doctor's appointment is about one hour, the 'processing time' is only about five minutes."

"OK, let's take a few minutes break and when we return we'll talk about the Define section of DMAIC," Karen said.

Chapter 16

The team members came back into the room after a short break. Keisha dropped a candy bar in front of Karen. "You may need the energy," she said.

"Thanks," Karen said. "Actually I love doing this!"

"And it's fun," Keisha said.

"Welcome back," Karen said. "Let me give an overview of DMAIC and then we'll jump right into the Define section. As I mentioned earlier, Six Sigma is a structured business tool for problem solving that relies heavily on meeting customer needs. At the heart of Six Sigma is DMAIC, which is an acronym for Define-Measure-Analyze-Improve-Control."

"Can you give us an explanation of each step?" Keisha asked.

"Sure thing," Karen said. "The Define section is where we Define the customer, their requirements, and the problem. Once complete, we move to Measure, where we measure the key variables of the process such as how long it takes to issue a permit. Then we Analyze the current process with tools such as process flow mapping. We then Improve the current process by looking for waste and modifying the process to meet the customer requirements. And finally, we put Control mechanisms in place, such as standardized work practices. This ensures that the process continues to meet the customer requirements in the future."

"You know that sounds like a lot," Cindy said, "but when you look at it the method is really quite simple. You define the problem, you measure the problem, you analyze the process, you improve the process, and then you set in place systems to keep the solution going."

"Great summary," Karen said. "Let's jump into the Define section. Everything in DMAIC must be focused on the customer and meeting their needs. So the first question we need to ask is, who is the customer for Development Services, and what are their needs?"

"It seems like the citizens of the City of Neal are our customers," Adam said.

"OK, that's a good start, but let's refine that even further. Is *every* citizen a customer?" Karen asked.

"I see where you are going with this," Patel said. "Every citizen is a *potential* customer, but considering that we are dealing with residential and commercial building permits, our actual customers are either homeowners, business owners, or contractors."

"Good," Karen said. "Let's break down these groups even further. Are they all represented equally when requesting a permit?"

"I can handle this one," Adam said. "Since I'm in the Safety division, at times I deal face-to-face with our applicants. Over time, I would say that about 80% of our permits go to homeowners, about 15% to contractors, and about 5% to business owners."

"OK, tell me more about each group?" Karen asked.

"Most of the homeowners are doing a project themselves without a contractor," Adam said, "such as adding a deck or building a shed. They have probably never requested a building permit before and they need a lot of hand holding from us. The contractors on the other hand deal with us on a routine basis, so they know the steps. And the business owners are a mixed bag. Some of the small mom and pop businesses are similar to the homeowners and have never requested a building permit before. The larger businesses or national chains generally have a staff person that knows the process to request a permit."

"And what about their technical skills for filing a permit?" Karen asked.

Adam chuckled. "Boy, I have seen everything from hand drawn sketches on the back of an envelope from the homeowners to sophisticated blueprints from the contractors. But the vast majority of the submissions come from homeowners who submit plans they drew at home either by hand or with a simple drawing software package."

"So you can see from this," Karen said, "we need to accommodate hand drawn applications as well as blueprints. Now that we have identified our customer and broke them down into groups, what are their requirements? In other words, what do they expect from us? A term for their expectations that's frequently used is the Voice-of-the-Customer or VOC."

"Tell us more about VOC, please," Brad said.

"It's the customer requirements for an efficient process," Karen said. "Remember, if you don't accurately identify the customer requirements you will not be successful at the end of the project."

"How do you determine the Voice-of-the-Customer?" Patel asked.

"There are a variety of methods," Karen said. "The simplest and most straightforward way is to simply ask the customer what they want. When you are interacting with them, just observe. Their body language and mannerism will tell you when they are frustrated and that can mean a problem."

"I've seen a lot of this at the front counter," Adam said.

"Other, more sophisticated methods are to use focus groups made up of permit applicants or send out a survey," Karen said. "Another method is to benchmark what other building permit agencies are offering. Look at other cities similar in size to the City of Neal. See how they handle the building permit process. What is their expected time to issue a permit? How do they account for differences with different groups applying for permits?"

"We actually did some benchmarking in the past," Brad said. "We found that similar-sized cities review permits and provide a response within fifteen business days for home renovations, twenty business days for new home construction, and twenty five business days for business permits."

"That's a lot faster than our sixty day turnaround," Cindy said.

"From my experience," Keisha said, "customers want a simple and easy to follow process. They don't want to fill out multiple applications. And they want an answer quickly."

"This is a good place to talk about our Charter," Karen said. "A Charter is a very important document as it outlines the project, provides a problem statement, provides expected outcomes, identifies team members and provides other important facts. It sets the stage for what a team is trying to accomplish over the next several weeks. Here is a Charter that I made up for our group. Let's talk through each point so you have a clear understanding."

Development Services Charter

Team Members: Keisha Wilson, Cindy Heinz, Tim Dresser, Patel Sami, Adam Thatcher, and Brad Able

Facilitator: Karen Spencer

Project Sponsor: Sam McConnell

Date: October 12

Problem Statement: Building Permits are averaging sixty days to be issued or denied.

Expected Outcome: Revise the process used by Development Services to meet the needs of our customers - which is to issue or deny a home renovation permit within fifteen business days, a new home construction permit within twenty days, and a commercial permit within twenty-five days.

Approach: Use DMAIC problem solving and Lean principles to shorten the time for a permit to be issued or denied.

Analysis Start: A customer submits a building permit application.

Analysis Stop: The permit is issued or denied.

Project Time Frame: Six to eight weeks with regularly scheduled meetings.

Stakeholders: Development Services Department, Engineering, Planning, Health, Safety, Water Quality, and the City of Neal

Customers: Home owners, business owners, and contractors

"At the top of the Project Charter," Karen said, "is the **title** of the project. Followed by the **team members, facilitator, sponsor** and **date**. In this case, Sam our City Manager, is our sponsor. And as sponsor, he's given us permission to proceed with this project. Next we list the **problem statement**. You don't need anything detailed here. Just a sentence or two as to why the team was formed. Our **expected outcome** is next. In our case it's to shorten the time to issue the permit to meet our customer's needs. We will use the fifteen days that Adam stated earlier as our goal. Our **approach** is our method for solving the problem. When we dig into the details of the problem, our methods may change. But suffice to say that we will be following the DMAIC method and applying Lean principles."

"Why do we list the analysis start and stop?" Keisha asked.

"It's always important to put parameters around the project," Karen said. "Otherwise things can quickly get out of hand and the project becomes too massive."

"I can relate to that," Brad said. "I've been on some projects that just kept getting bigger and bigger to the point that we didn't know what problem we were trying to solve."

"That's right," Karen said. "Without clearly defined start and stop analysis points things get out of hand quickly."

"And so does your effectiveness," Brad said.

"In our project," Karen said, "we'll start the analysis when a customer submits an application for a permit to Development Services. We'll end it when they have either issued or denied the permit. Sound correct?"

The team members nodded.

"The last three sections of the charter," Karen said, "are the anticipated **time frame** for project completion, the **stakeholders**, and the **customers**."

"Karen, can you define a little better who the stakeholders are and who the customers are?" Adam asked.

"Sure," Karen said. "Stakeholders are people or organizations who are highly invested in this process. In our case, the Department of Development Services, and the Divisions of Engineering, Planning, Water Quality, Safety and Environmental Health all have a part in reviewing a permit application. That's why we have a representative from each here with us today. In addition, the City of Neal is also a stakeholder as our reputation is at stake."

"And how are customers different?" Adam asked.

"Customers are the people that consume the output of the process," Karen said. "In our case it is the homeowners, business owners, and contractors who are asking for a permit."

"But isn't Development Services also a customer?" Tim asked. "I mean, they will be using this process day-in and day-out. So shouldn't we consider their needs as well?"

"That's not exactly correct," Karen said. "If you considered the needs of Development Services, you would be missing the needs of the true customer."

"How?" Adam asked. "How do we know who the true customer is?"

"There's an easy method to help you differentiate between a customer and a stakeholder," Karen said. "And that is to ask this question: If the group that you believed to be the customer went away, would there still be a need for this process?"

The group thought about Karen's words for a minute.

"For example," Karen said, "if Development Services went away, would there still be a need for issuing permits?"

"Yes, there would still be a need," Adam said, "because the law states that when a person wants to build a new house, they still need a permit whether Development Services is here or not."

"That's right," Karen said. "And, since there is still a need for the process of issuing permit, then Development Services is *not* the customer of the process, but they are a stakeholder."

"So if the homeowners, business owners, and contractors went away," Keisha said, "then the need for issuing permits would go away as well."

"That's right," Karen said. "If there were no homeowners, business owners, or contractors, then there would be no need to issue permits. That makes them the *customers* of this process. And as service providers, we need to make the process meet *their requirements*."

"Does the charter make sense to everyone?" Karen asked.

Everyone nodded.

"What's the next step?" Tim asked.

"We'll be meeting early next week to discuss the Measure phase of DMAIC," Karen said. "However, to prepare for that meeting, I have some homework for you. Between now and then, do some research on the project numbers. List how long permits have taken to issue. How long they sit at each department. How many are approved or denied. Think also about the Voice-of-the-Customer. Ask if we are meeting the customer needs. In the measure phase we need to write down numbers so we get a true sense of how long the steps in the permit process takes. Without this we will not know if we improved the process or not."

"We've got some work ahead of us," Keisha said.

"You do, but in the long run, it will make much less work for you and the people you supervise. OK, see you next week," Karen said.

"Thanks, Karen," Cindy said, "I'm excited about where this can lead."

Chapter 17

Sam and Laura loved their Sunday morning breakfasts. They were there to eat, hang out and enjoy each other's company. Sam walked into the kitchen in his worn sweatpants, a T-shirt and flip-flops. Laura stood at the stove. Sam came up behind her, puts his arms around her and kissed the back of her neck.

"Honey, can you get me some eggs from the refrigerator?" Laura asked.

"How many do you want?"

"Give me four, I'm going to make some French toast," Laura said.

Sam took out the eggs and handed them to her. "What's your plan for later today?"

"I'm getting together with my friend Julie for a walk around the lake," Laura said. "The fall colors are in full splendor. Want to join us?"

"That's not a bad idea," Sam said. "I have a few things to do on the rental this morning, but I could join you in the afternoon. How about two this afternoon?"

"That should probably work," Laura said.

"Great, then count me in," Sam said. "How is your sister doing?"

"Unfortunately, not so good," Karen said. "She may need to go to the hospital for some out-patient procedure next week. In fact, I should call her now to get the latest."

"While you do that, I'm going to grab the newspaper from the driveway," Sam said.

"When you get back," Laura said, "can you keep an eye on the French toast? I may be a few minutes."

"No problem," Sam said and went out the door.

* * *

The smoke alarm shriek brought Laura running back into the kitchen. A thin layer of black smoke clung to the ceiling. The French toast was burning.

"Sam! I thought that I asked you to watch the food!" Laura shouted. Sam was nowhere in sight. She turned off the stove, put the smoking pan into the sink, and opened a few windows to air out the kitchen. Just then, Sam entered the room. His face was pale white.

"Sam where were you?" Laura asked. "I asked you to watch the stove and now breakfast is ruined."

Sam looked flustered. "What?"

"Sam, the toast almost caught fire! Where were you?"

Sam held up the front page of the paper. "Look, here's today's headline; 'City Government Gets a Grade of F.'"

"I can't believe this," Sam said. He sat at the kitchen table and put the paper in front of him. Laura sat next to him.

"How could they do this to us . . . and *why* did they do this?" Sam asked. "I was never even asked to comment on this story!"

Laura put her hand on Sam's shoulder. "What does the story say?"

Sam started to read. "Citizens are complaining . . . services not keeping pace with demand . . . morale among city staff at an all-time low . . . Who the hell wrote this story?"

"Honey don't worry, nobody reads this paper anyway," Laura said.

Sam pointed to the article. "Where did this information come from?" He felt his chest tightening. "Look they interviewed Trisha and the new City Council Members. Why the hell didn't they contact me?"

"Honey I'm sorry that this happened," Laura said.

Sam grabbed his cell phone. "I've got to call Carl." He dialed. "Carl, it's Sam, did you see the paper this morning?"

"I did," Carl said.

"Did you know about this story?" Sam asked.

"No," Carl said. "It's all new to me."

"What prompted the paper to write a story about us?" Sam asked.

"I don't know," Carl said.

"Why in the hell did the paper interview the Council Members and not come to us before they publish this garbage?" Sam said. "This is bad Carl, real bad. We've been vilified. When people read this kind of crap they believe it whether it's true or not. Then their minds are made up."

"We'll need to go into damage control mode," Carl said. "Maybe I can talk with the reporter and request a meeting so that we can give him our side of the story."

"Go ahead and try that," Sam said. "They may not be receptive to the idea, but it's worth a try."

"I'll do what I can," Carl said.

"Thanks for your help as always," Sam said and hung up. He stared straight ahead. "Damn."

Chapter 18

On Tuesday morning, Karen entered the conference room and saw the DMAIC team already seated at the table and eager to begin. "Welcome back everyone. Are there any questions or comments before we get started?"

"Why the emphasis on numbers for the measure stage?" Keisha asked.

Cindy raised her hand. "I can answer this one."

"Go for it," Karen said.

"I mentioned at our last meeting," Cindy said, "that I had some Six Sigma training. Our instructor told us that goals needed to be expressed in numbers. He wouldn't let us just state the problem with fuzzy language such as 'the process is taking too long' or 'the customers are not happy'. Without numbers to guide us we leave too much to interpretation."

"Thanks, Cindy. That's a great explanation," Karen said. "With Six Sigma, data rules. Numbers and data are keys to a successful project. And since we defined our goal as fifteen business days, we need to measure all of the attributes of the process. Let's start with some simple metrics such as the number of applications submitted each year."

"I've got those figures," Brad said. "Over the last three years, we have been averaging about 4,000 permit applications every year."

"And are they evenly spread out throughout the year?" Karen asked.

"No, since we are dealing with building permits," Brad said, "we receive almost 50%, or about 2,000 applications during the summer months of June, July, and August. The other 2,000 are split over the other nine months."

"It's always good to consider seasonal variation when redefining a new process," Karen said.

"There certainly are lots of things to measure," Patel said.

"I agree," Karen said. "But it's important for us to focus on the important metrics of the process. What do you think some of those are?"

"Here's my list," Tim said. "I think that we need to define how long it takes to issue a permit, how long the application sits within each division for review, and what are the lead and process times within each division."

"That's a good start," Karen said. "Any other ideas?"

"I went a bit further," Brad said. "I broke down the permit process depending upon the application type. For example, the review times are much different for a simple house addition, such as a patio deck, versus building a new custom home."

"And business permits are quite involved," Keisha said. Everyone nodded in agreement.

"In the Measure phase of DMAIC," Karen said, "we want to analyze the performance of the current system and then compare it to the customer needs. Let's start off with the most important measurement of the permit issuing process—which is how long does it usually take to issue or deny a permit?"

"I've got a good handle on those numbers," Brad said. "The average time was fifty-seven days. I looked at all permit applications over the past two years. As I mentioned earlier, the simple permits for a single family renovation took about thirty-nine days, custom homes took about sixty-five days, and the business permits took around ninety days, but the overall average for all permits was fifty-seven days."

"I'm glad that you broke the numbers down like that," Karen said. "Because it may be appropriate to list three separate promise dates broken out by renovations, custom homes and businesses."

Karen wrote the permit times on the conference room white board.

Permit Type	Average Number of Days
Renovations	39
Custom Homes	65
Businesses	90
Average for all permits	57

"Does everyone agree with these numbers?" Karen asked.

"They sound realistic to me," Keisha said. Others nodded in agreement.

"Two things to remember when you are calculating the numbers," Karen said. "The first is to do your best estimate based on the data that you have, but don't get too hung up in trying to calculate the 'perfect' number. When you think about it, it doesn't matter much if the average number of days is fifty-seven or sixty-one. The second thing to remember when calculating these numbers is to look at what happens 80% of the time. Don't include the unusual situations in your analysis."

"And I took that into consideration," Brad said. "I found several business permits that took almost six months to issue. I didn't include them in the calculation as they were very unusual situations."

"Good," Karen said. "We just want to consider what happens the majority of the time. So what are some other metrics that we should be listing?"

"I determined that only about 5% of all permit applications are ultimately denied," Adam said. "Some do require additional information from the customer or slight modifications, but almost all eventually make it through the system."

"I looked at how long the permits sit in Engineering," Tim said, "and how long it takes to actually process them."

"Let's clarify lead time and processing time again," Karen said. "The 'lead time' is the time that the application sits in Engineering and is measured from when a permit application *arrives* at your office until it *leaves* your office. The 'processing time' is how long someone at Engineering is actually *working* on the application."

"Yep, that's how I calculated these numbers," Tim said. "I found that on average, our lead time is seven days, but the processing time is only about six hours."

"So that means," Karen said, "that only six hours of 'Value Added' activity was applied to the permit application over a seven day period."

"I'm embarrassed to say that's correct," Tim said. "Between waiting in the queue, moving around within our office, a review by the engineering technician, and a final approval by the engineering manager, the application was with us for on average seven days. However, when we looked at how much time was spent actually working on the permit application it came out to only about six hours."

"Let's go around the table," Karen said. "Please give me the lead and processing times for your division. Adam, let's start with you."

"Our lead time is twelve days," Adam said, "and the processing time is five hours."

"And your times, Patel?" Karen asked.

"At Water Quality," Patel said, "our total lead time from start to finish is eleven days and the total processing time is seven hours."

"Keisha, how about you?" Karen asked.

"At Health the average time that a permit was in our division was fourteen days," Keisha said. "And I'm *really* embarrassed to say this—our actual processing time is only two hours."

"Two hours!" Patel said. "That's not much time at all, and yet it takes fourteen days from start to finish in your department?"

"I know," Keisha said. "It is embarrassing, but it's also reality."

"Don't worry," Karen said. "In the Improve phase of DMAIC we'll get that lead time way down. Cindy, how about the Planning division?"

"We're at eight days for lead time," Cindy said, "and two hours for processing time."

"Thanks everyone," Karen said. "These numbers are very important. Because if we didn't have them, we'd never know much the process improved when we're finished. Let's review what we discovered in the measure phase. We found out that adding up the lead time for the five divisions our total is fifty-two days."

Department	Lead Time	Processing Time
Engineering	7 days	6 hours
Environmental Health	14 days	2 hours
Planning	8 days	2 hours
Water Quality	11 days	7 hours
Safety	12 days	5 hours
TOTAL	**52 days**	**22 hours**

"And that's pretty close to the fifty-seven days I estimated," Brad said.

"So we can probably trust that number," Karen said. "But when you look at the fifty-two days, only about twenty-two hours of actual work was performed on each application. Where did all of the other time go?"

"There was a lot of waiting at our office," Cindy said.

"Ours as well," Keisha said.

"Good," Karen said. "Remember that Lean is *not* about trying to speed up the twenty-two 'Value-Added' hours spent working on the application. It is about eliminating the fifty some days of waiting, motion, transportation, and other waste inherent in our current process."

The conference room was silent as the team all nodded.

"Does our current performance meet the needs of our users?" Karen asked.

"I think we can clearly state *no*," Patel said, "given that we are averaging sixty days to issue a permit, this does not meet their needs."

Others shook their heads in agreement.

"That sets the stage for next week as we move into the Analyze phase of DMAIC," Karen said. "Give yourselves a hand for a job well done."

The team applauded, gave thumbs up to each other and the meeting ended.

Chapter 19

It was a quiet Friday afternoon in the Neal government offices. A three-day weekend was only hours away and many of the staff skipped out early or took today off as a vacation day. Sam was working at his desk.

"Sam, Larry from Development Services is here to see you," Patty said.

Sam checked his calendar. There was no appointment with Larry. "OK, send him in."

Larry entered Sam's office. He looked grim.

"Hi Larry, what brings you here today?" Sam asked.

"It's Karen," Larry said. "That lady is causing quite a commotion in my department."

"What do you mean?" Sam asked.

"This process improvement project, that DMAIC thing."

"And what's your problem with that?" Sam asked.

"It's taking a lot of time from my people," Larry said. "And you know that I am short staffed. I just can't afford for people to be in meetings when we have a backlog of work that we can't get to."

"Why can't you get to that work?" Sam asked.

"Because I have too much work and not enough people!" Larry snapped.

"Do you think if those six people on the team," Sam said, "stopped the DMAIC exercise and 'went back to work' as you called it, would you be able to catch-up with your backlog?"

"Probably not," Larry said. "We have too much to do."

"So Larry, consider this," Sam said. "You don't want to change anything, but if you don't change, then you will never get rid of your backlog. Did you ever consider that maybe your process is too complicated?"

"Our system is not too complicated," Larry said angrily. "I have it set the way I like it, and I don't want anyone messing with it."

"Larry, let's calm this discussion down a bit," Sam said. "We have to realize that we aren't meeting the needs of our customers right now. They're not happy with us, the City Council is not happy with us. As human beings, we don't always like change. It scares us. But it's something that we have to do and we must embrace change."

"Sam, I have been in that department for over twenty years," Larry said. "Don't you think that I know the process better than anyone else does?"

"No argument there, Larry," Sam said. "You know it better than anyone. But to improve, sometimes we may need to take a fresh look at things, you know, get a new perspective. Are you willing to give Karen's ideas a try?"

"I would if I thought that they had a chance to succeed," Larry said. "Look Sam, this DMAIC stuff is just not right for our organization. Lean and efficiency are great for companies that make stuff, but we're the government, we don't manufacture anything."

"Why don't you think Lean applies to us?" Sam asked.

"Because we are offering a service, not producing a product," Larry said.

"But you are 'manufacturing' a product," Sam said. "And the product is the permits that you issue to homeowners, contractors, and business owners. Lean applies to you even though you don't have machinery in your department."

"I still don't see the connection," Larry said.

Sam rapped his knuckles on the table. "Look Larry, to produce this table, it took raw materials such as wood and screws and a process to assemble it. And it's in the best interest of the manufacturer to use the minimal amount of resources and time to assemble that table. Wouldn't you agree with that?"

"Yes," Larry said. "Because the customer wants it at the lowest price."

"Right," Sam said. "And *your* customers are the homeowners, contractors, and business owners. They want *you* to produce their approved permit using the minimal amount of time and resources. They want it at the lowest price, just like the buyer for this table."

"I hear you, but I'm not convinced," Larry said.

"Larry, it's natural to be a bit skeptical of something new," Sam said. "I just ask that you let Karen do her work. Then we can look at the results. Besides, the holiday weekend is upon us. How about you and I go out and get some pizza right now?"

"You buying?" Larry asked.

"Of course."

Chapter 20

On Tuesday, Karen entered the conference room to find that all of the DMAIC team members were already sitting around the table.

"Good morning," Karen said. "I hope that everyone had fun over the long holiday weekend."

"When I come back from those long weekends," Patel said, "I tend to forget what I do for a living."

Tim grinned. "Well you don't do much around here."

"All right, all right," Karen said. "Today we move into the Analyze phase. Here we determine why we are not meeting customer requirements. And we do that by breaking the process down into small discrete components. This allows us to see what is happening. Think of this phase like opening the hood of your car when the engine doesn't start. You are getting under the surface and looking at the details. Sound OK?"

"Is this Analyze phase even necessary?" Tim asked. "We spoke before about how the movement of the paper files between divisions is slowing us down. Couldn't we just make the file electronic, e-mail it to each other, and keep the same process flow?"

"Then you would have a sub-optimal process," Karen said. "We all agree that an electronic file will shorten our delivery time, but there are lots of other wastes in the current process that aren't apparent until you analyze the flow. Please hold that thought until we finish with the Analysis phase."

"OK, then let's see what other wastes we can find," Tim said.

"As a starting point," Karen said, "we have an existing value stream map from Development Services. However, this map is very high level."

"How detailed should we get with this new map?" Patel asked.

"Detailed enough," Karen said, "that we can identify the waste steps in the process. I've found that if you build a process flow map with swim lanes you will be able to identify waste."

"How many swim lanes should there be?" Patel asked.

"There are five divisions," Cindy said, "so I would say five swim lanes."

"What about the person at the front counter?" Tim asked. "Shouldn't they be represented by a swim lane also?"

"And don't forget about the customer," Brad said.

"I agree with both comments," Karen said. "We should have seven swim lanes to represent the five divisions, the front counter, and the customer."

"The easiest way I've found to map a process," Karen said, "is to use different color sticky notes and place them on a white board. Sticky notes are great because we can easily move them around the board without much trouble. And by putting the sticky notes on a white board, we can draw lines with a marker to indicate how the process flows. For today's exercise, we will use yellow sticky notes to represent a process, the pink ones to represent the start and end points, and the light blue notes to indicate a decision. And since a decision can have a 'yes' or 'no' answer, we will rotate the light blue notes forty-five degrees to form a diamond shape. Does this make sense to everyone?"

"Let's get going," Adam said.

"Let me start," Karen said, "by first passing out the value stream map that Brad developed."

Karen passed out paper copies of the map.

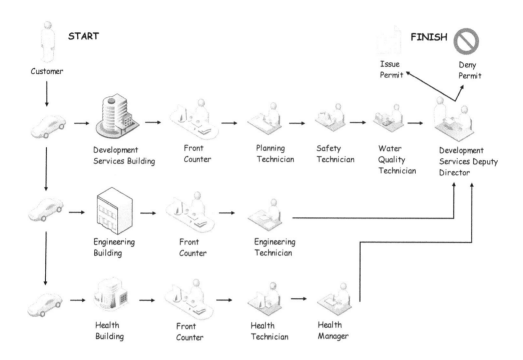

"Brad, does this map still accurately reflect the big picture flow?" Karen asked.

"Yep, that's the process we use today," Brad said.

"Our value stream map is very high level," Karen said. "It's like looking at a state road map. You'll see the highways and major roads, but not the individual streets. And for us to find and eliminate waste, we need to get down to the street level. Think of it as going from a state road map to a city map with all of the streets and alleys listed. When we are at this level, we can find the waste. The map that we'll produce today is called a process flow map with swim lanes."

"Also, we're mapping what's called the 'current state'. Meaning that we are only depicting how the process is done today. We will use the 80/20 rule and only map out what happens 80% of the time. Don't worry about the anomalies of what happens the other 20% of the time. And finally, we have three distinct processes from the customer's viewpoint. Keisha what are those?"

"First," Keisha said, "the customer comes to the Development Services office and applies for a permit with the Planning, Safety, and Water Quality divisions. Then they drive over to Engineering to apply for their permit, and finally, they drive over to Health for their permit."

"That sounds right," Karen said. "To simplify the flow, let's map out *three different* process flows to represent the three locations that the customer must drive to. Brad, what is the action at the Development Services office that starts your process flow?"

"The process starts," Brad said, "when a customer goes to the Development Services building and submits a permit application to Planning, Safety, and Water Quality."

"Right," Karen said. "I'll write 'application submitted' on a pink note and stick it in the customer's swim lane," Karen completed this action. "What's next?" Karen asked.

Development Services – Current State	
Customer	Application Submitted
Front Counter	
Planning	
Safety	
Water	

"The person at the front counter," Brad said, "will accept the application and collect the money. The fee will vary depending upon if it's a residential or commercial application."

Karen took a yellow sticky note, wrote 'accept application and collect money' on it and posted it in the front counter swim lane.

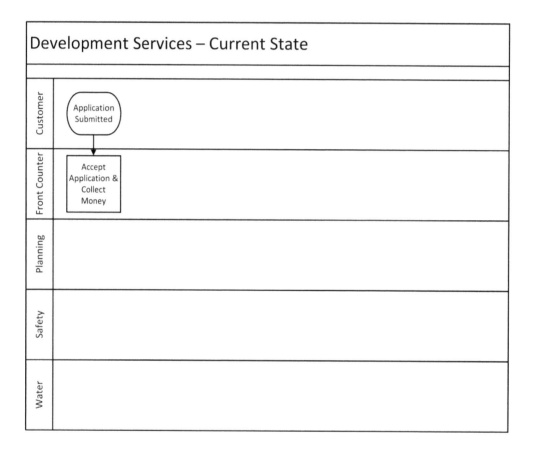

"To show that the process is moving from the pink note to this yellow note," Karen said, "I'll draw an arrow with a magic marker indicating the direction of flow." Karen drew the arrow on the white board.

"OK, what's the next step?" Karen asked.

"The front counter person walks the application over to the Planning Department for their review," Brad said.

"To represent the process of walking," Karen said, "I'll put a sticky note with the phrase 'walk to planning' in the front counter swim lane."

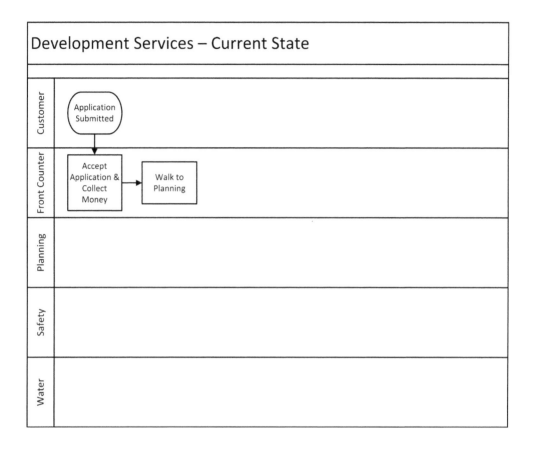

"OK, Cindy, you are in Planning, what happens next?" Karen asked.

"We collect about five applications before we start looking at them," Cindy said. "That way, one of our planning reviewers has a set of applications to review all at once." Karen wrote 'wait for five applications' on a yellow sticky and posted it in the Planning swim lane.

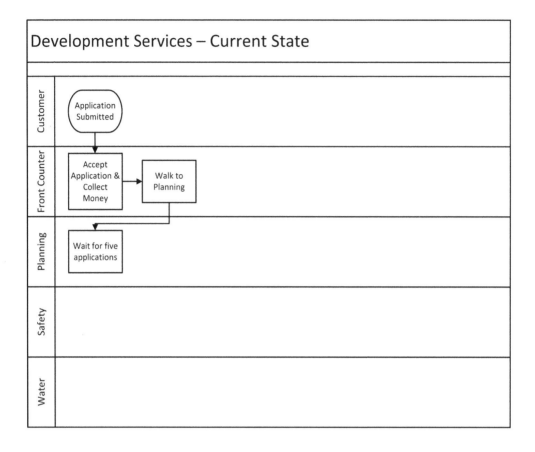

"Why do you do that?" Patel asked. "Why don't you look at them as soon as they get to your desk?"

"We want the planner to stay focused on the task," Cindy said.

"I know, but —" Patel said, but was interrupted by Karen.

"No criticism," Karen said. "When you map a process, you only look at how you do the *current process*. What Planning is doing is called 'batching'. And whenever you batch something you have the waste of 'waiting' and the waste of 'inventory'. If you think about it, files number one through four are just waiting for the fifth file. And it's a waste of 'inventory' as you have too many files, and these extra files are adding no value. If we have a better idea, let's note that in the 'action item' list and look into that idea at a later time." Karen went to another white board and wrote 'Action Items' on the top of the board and wrote 'Look into eliminating batching applications at Planning.'

Action Items
1) Look into eliminating batching applications at Planning

"It's a good idea," Karen said. "Let's just note it now and discuss it at a later time."

"Others refer to your 'action item' list as the 'parking lot'" Adam said. "It's where you place an item now and delve into the specifics at a later time."

"Yes, that's correct," Karen said. "Back to the process flow map. Let's review . . . we have a customer submit an application, the front counter person collects the money, they walk it to Planning, and Planning waits for five applications to accumulate before they start the review process."

"Cindy, now that five applications are there, what do you do?" Karen asked.

"The planner opens each file," Cindy said, "to see if the application was filled out completely and if all of the supporting documentation is there."

"This is a decision step," Karen said. "I'll use a blue sticky note and write 'Is application complete?' I'll put it on the board, but at a forty-five degree angle."

"Please continue Cindy," Karen said.

"If the application is missing information or documents," Cindy said, "then the planner will note this and call the applicant asking for more information. If everything is there, then the planner starts the review process."

"Let's show this graphically on the board," Karen said. She wrote on a yellow note, 'obtain more information' and put it in the customer swim lane. She then drew a line connecting one corner of the blue note to the yellow note and wrote 'NO' next to that line. Next, Karen used another yellow note and wrote 'review application' and put it in the Planning swim lane. She drew another line starting on a different corner of the blue note and connected it to the yellow note and wrote 'YES' next to that line.

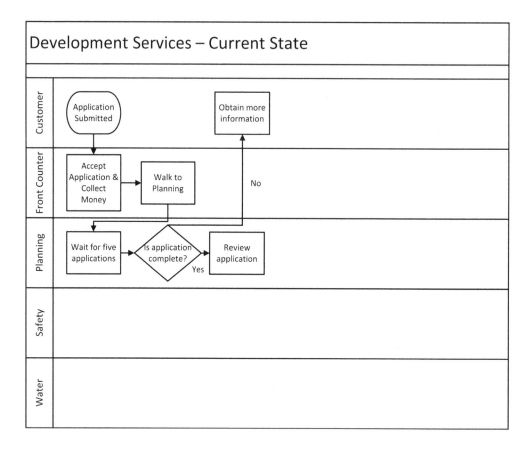

Development Services – Current State

"You can see that the blue note is a decision point," Karen said. "And we can branch the process flow depending upon the answer?"

"So the process can flow in one of two directions?" Patel asked.

"That's right," Karen said, "depending upon if the application is complete or not, the flow may change. OK, what's next Cindy?"

"If the application is complete," Cindy said, "the planner reviews the application and determines what the customer wants. The planner will refer to a land use guide and note what type of zoning is allowed in that area. The planner then decides if they will approve or deny the application. If the applicant's request is allowed, then we stamp the application 'Approved by Planning' with the date and then forward the application to the Safety department."

"What if the application is denied?" Tim asked.

"Then we will stamp 'Denied by Planning,'" Cindy said, "with the date, note the reasons why, and then forward the application back to the customer."

"The 'review application' is a 'Value Added' step," Karen said. "The planner is 'changing the form and function' of the application by comparing it with existing zoning regulations. They will either accept it or deny it. This is how our current state value stream map looks so far."

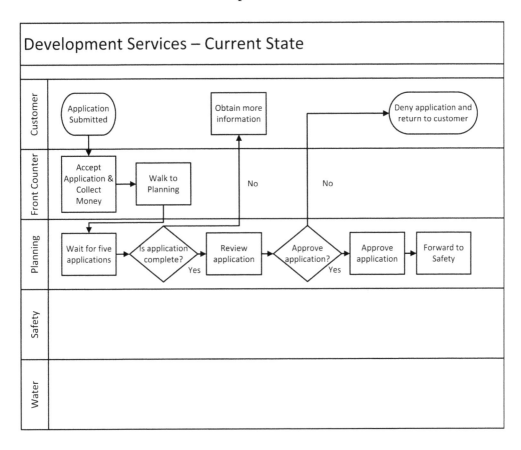

"OK, Adam," Karen said, "the application has been approved by Planning and now has been forwarded to Safety. Is the application reviewed immediately?"

"We usually start reviewing it by the next working day," Adam said.

"So there is probably a 'wait' step in there," Karen said. Adam nodded his head in agreement.

"Now, what do you do?" Karen asked.

"We follow a similar pattern as planning, but we're not batching them," Adam said. "Every application that we receive is routed to one of our Safety technicians. We look to see what type of structure the applicant wants to build and then review the relevant building codes."

"Is there a decision step in there?" Karen asked.

"Yes, once we've completed our review," Adam said, "we'll either deny the application and send it back to the applicant, or approve it and forward it on to Water Quality."

Karen drew the new process chart and asked if everyone was in agreement. The group studied the flow and agreed that the flow was accurate.

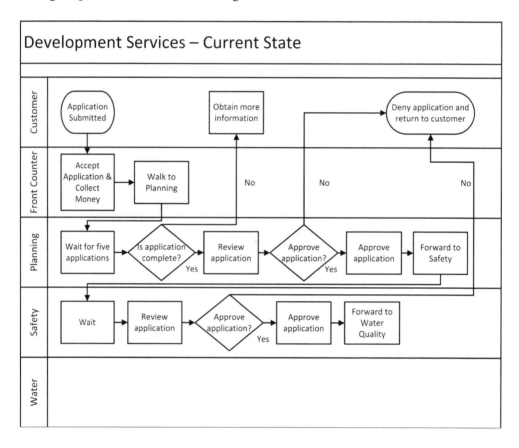

"Patel," Karen said, "you receive the file from Safety, what do you do?"

"One of our technicians," Patel said, "will review the application for water and sewer connections. If there were no sewer connections in the area, then the applicant would need to install a septic tank and leech field. Sometime, we need to go out into the field but most of the time, we can refer to our maps and charts in the office."

"And if the application is denied?" Karen asked.

"Then we forward it back to the customer and ask for additional details," Patel said.

"And if the application is approved?" Karen asked.

"Then we walk it over to Brad in Development Services," Patel said. "And he waits for the mating file to be returned from Engineering and Health."

Karen finalized the new process chart and asked if it was accurate. The group agreed that the flow was accurate.

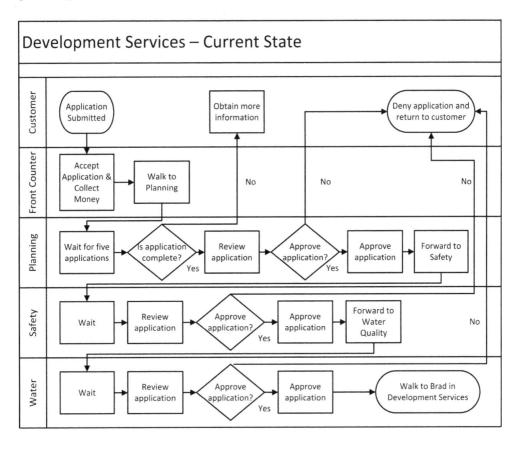

"Now let's continue," Karen said, "with mapping the Engineering process flow."

Turning to Tim, Karen asked, "What starts your process?"

"We start," Tim said, "when the customer comes into our office and fills out another application."

"Is it the same application," Karen asked, "that was used by Planning, Safety, and Water Quality?"

"No," Tim said. "The customer needs to fill out a new application. At Engineering, we're concerned if the property is in a flood plain, so we don't need the details requested by the other departments. But we do have additional questions for the applicant."

"That seems like a waste of over-production on the customer's side," Adam said, "asking them to fill out a new application doesn't seem to be in the customer's best interests."

"I agree," Karen said. "Let's put the idea of having only one universal application on the action list." Karen added this idea on the action list for investigation at a future time.

Action Items
1) Look into eliminating batching applications at Planning
2) Develop one universal application for all five divisions

"Once the application is complete," Tim said, "we ask the customer to show their receipt. This proves that they've already paid for the permit when they submitted the application with Planning, Safety, and Water Quality."

"At one point in time," Keisha said, "we required the customer to pay once at Planning, Safety, and Water Quality, again at Engineering, and again at Health. Boy did we get a lot of complaints from our customers."

"What did you do?" Karen asked.

"We changed the policy to require only one payment," Keisha said, "and then have the customer show the receipt to the other divisions."

"That's great," Karen said. "There are two lessons to learn from this. First, be aware of customer complaints. They are generally a sign that the process isn't working properly. And the second lesson to remember is that you have the ability to change a process that doesn't work. Don't accept that cliché of 'that's the way we have always done things around here.' Be willing to take the initiative and change things."

"And once we changed our process," Keisha said, "the complaints disappeared."

"I'm not surprised," Karen said. "Tim, please go on with the process flow."

"Once we have their application," Tim said, "we walk the file over to an Engineering technician for a review."

"I'll put a 'walk application' on a sticky note," Karen said.

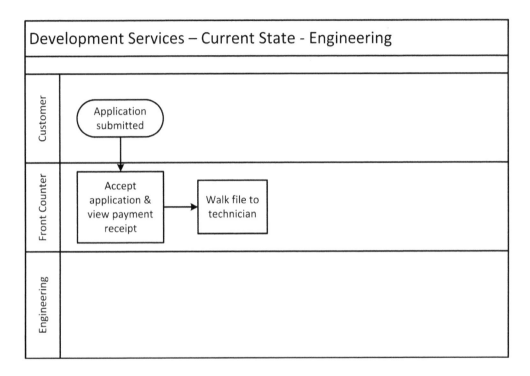

"Once the Engineering Technician receives the file, he'll do an inspection to see if the file is complete. If yes, he'll forward it on for a review. If the file is not complete, he'll send it back to the customer."

"Let's document this on the map," Karen said.

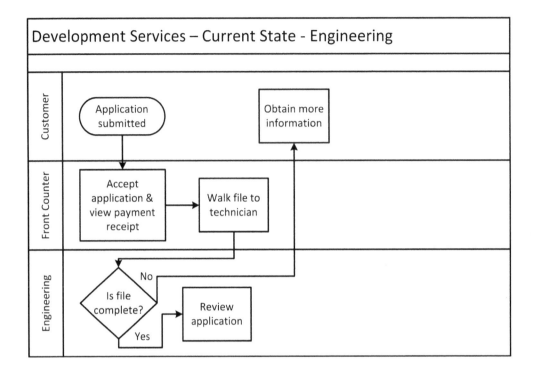

"As with the other departments," Tim said, "we do a review of the proposed project and either accept or deny it."

"I'll add a blue sticky note," Karen said, "to represent this decision. And also a pink note to indicate the end of the process. One will state, 'deny the application' and the other will state 'forward to Development Services.'"

"Tim, does this look accurate?" Karen asked.

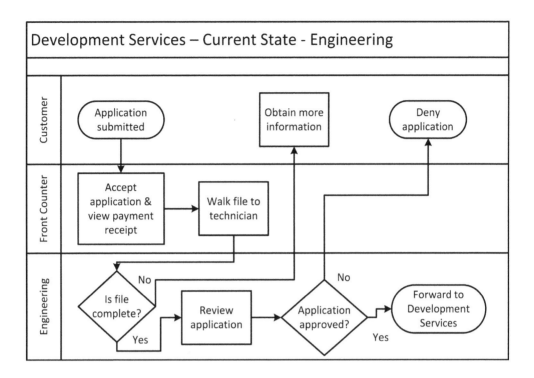

"Yes," Tim said. "It's correct."

"The final step that the customer must do to obtain a permit," Karen said, "is driving to the Environmental Health department."

"At Health," Keisha said, "we follow the same review procedure as Engineering. And I also agree that we should combine the Health application into the one universal application. I've certainly heard my share of complaints from customers when we ask them to fill out a third application."

"Great," Karen said. "We'll look into a universal application in more detail in the future. But first, let me put up some sticky notes to represent your process at Health." Karen added the sticky notes to the white board and drew arrows to indicate the flow.

"Keisha does this look correct?"

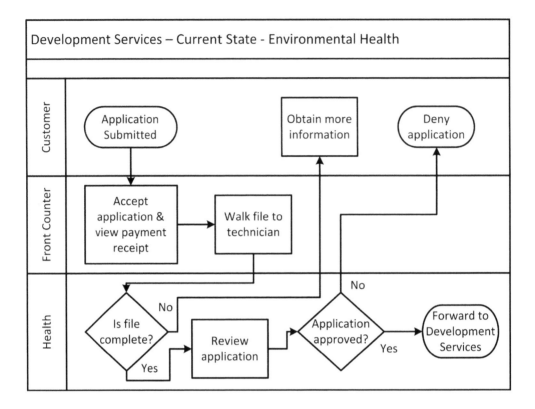

"Yes it does," Keisha said. "Except we have one additional approval step. Remember I said a few meetings ago that I need my supervisor to sign off on all completed applications."

"And if I remember correctly," Karen said, "you stated that your supervisor automatically signed off on all applications as you have more technical knowledge then she does."

"That's right," Keisha said. "I'll talk with my supervisor soon and see if we can eliminate this step."

"Should we put that on the Action Item list?" Patel asked.

"Great idea," Karen said and she added it to the list.

Action Items
1) Look into eliminating batching applications at Planning
2) Develop one universal application for all five divisions
3) Eliminate the approval step at Environmental Health

"Since the current process includes this approval step," Karen said, "let's indicate it on the flow chart. And does your Supervisor approve the file immediately?"

"No," Keisha said. "I walk the file over and place it on her desk. I usually get the signed file back the next day."

"I'll document these steps," Karen said.

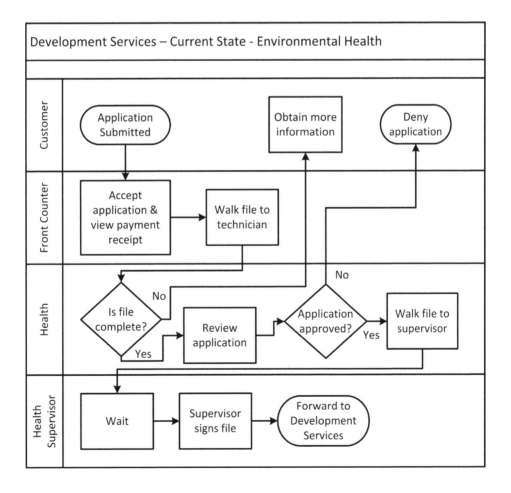

"Keisha, does this now represent the approval step?" Karen asked.

"Yes it does."

"OK, the final step," Karen said, "is for Brad to collect the three separate files at Development Services. Brad, please tell us what you do."

"I have my assistant," Brad said, "collect all of the incoming files. When all three files for the same application arrive, he puts them on my desk. I review the comments and if everyone is in agreement, we issue the permit."

"Let me draw this out," Karen said and proceeded to draw the process flow. "Does this look accurate?"

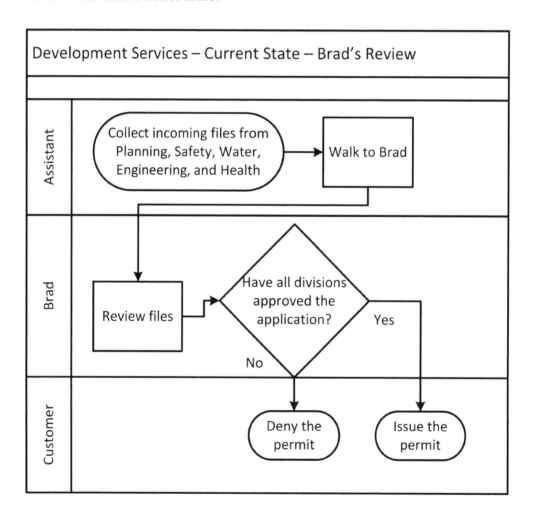

"It does," Brad said.

"Great job everyone," Karen said. "Let's take a break and when we come back we can start labeling the steps as either 'Value Added', 'Required', or 'Waste'.

Chapter 21

The team returned from their short break.

"Welcome back," Karen said. "In the first part of the meeting, we broke down the high level value stream map into a process flow map with swim lanes. The reason for this exercise is to give us additional detail on the process."

"It really wasn't that hard," Cindy said. "We all know our own processes as we use them every day, so documenting it didn't seem that bad."

"It's not," Karen said. "And the reason you were selected to be on the DMAIC team is that you all have first-hand experience with your own individual processes."

"Where do we go from here?" Adam asked.

"When I started today's meeting," Karen said, "I mentioned that our purpose in the Analysis phase was to understand why we are not meeting our customer requirements. When you look at the new swim lane flow charts, can we see why we aren't meeting those requirements?"

Adam raised his hand, "Looking at the four process maps, I realize how many times we used words like 'walking', 'forwarding' and 'waiting'."

"I agree," Keisha said. "It seems like we are spending more time moving the file around then we are doing any work on it."

"Great observation," Karen said. "Words like 'waiting' and 'walking' are what kind of steps?"

"Waste," Brad said. "They didn't add any value to the end product."

"Exactly," Karen said. "Let's look at the process flow maps we just produced and identify each step as either 'Value Added', 'Required', or 'Waste'. Who can give me a quick definition of these?"

Cindy raised her hand.

"Go on Cindy," Karen said.

"The 'Value Added' steps change the form or function," Cindy said, "and are something that the customer wants us to do. A 'Required' step may not change the form or function, but is something that we have to do, and 'Waste' steps add no value."

"Perfect. Thanks Cindy," Karen said. "Everyone study the first process flow swim lane map that we produced for Planning, Safety, and Water. Let's look at each step and identify it as either 'Value Added', 'Required', or 'Waste'.

"The first oval," Patel said, "which is 'Application Submitted' by the customer, seems to be a 'Value Added' step."

"I agree," Karen said. "It changed the form and function, as before the application was with the customer and now it is with Development Services."

"The next step," Patel said, "which is 'Accepting Application and Collecting Money' didn't add any value, but is required, as the customer needs to pay for the permit."

"I agree," Karen said. "Keep going, you're doing great."

"The next two steps," Patel said, "seem to be 'Waste' steps. As we just mentioned, walking the file and waiting for more files didn't change the status of the application."

"Great job Patel," Karen said. "To designate each step, I'll print 'VA' for Value Added, 'R' for Required, and 'W' for Waste on each step." Karen added these to the flow chart on the white board.

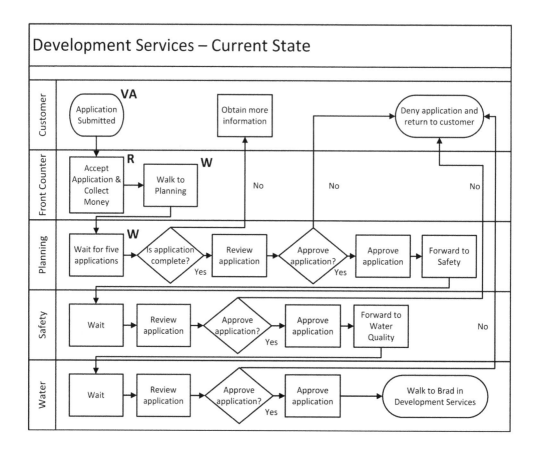

"What about the next step, which is a decision step?" Adam asked. "It doesn't seem to be adding any value, but it's not a Waste step either."

"Doesn't that make it a 'Required' step," Keisha said.

"I would agree," Tim said. "We do need to determine if the file is complete, so it's required."

"But shouldn't we be doing this step earlier on in the process?" Cindy asked.

"What does everyone think?" Karen asked.

"We should be checking if the file is complete," Brad said, "when we *accept* the application at the front counter. There's no reason to wait and check the file after the customer is gone."

"Why don't you do that now?" Karen asked.

"Because the front counter person isn't trained properly," Brad said.

"That's a waste of 'non-utilized' people," Cindy said.

"Boy, you guys are on it!" Karen said with a smile. "Do you see how easy this is once you break down the process? Let me add a 'W' to the decision step. It is a Waste step because it should have been done initially. What about the 'obtain more information step'? What type of step is that?"

"It's waste," Patel said. "The customer is providing us with additional information on their application, but this should have already been done. A properly trained front counter person would have eliminated this step."

"Let's add that idea to the action list," Karen said.

Action Items
1) Look into eliminating batching applications at Planning
2) Develop one universal application for all five divisions
3) Eliminate the approval step at Environmental Health
4) Train the front counter person to check if the application is complete at the front counter

"Let me also update the process flow map," Karen said.

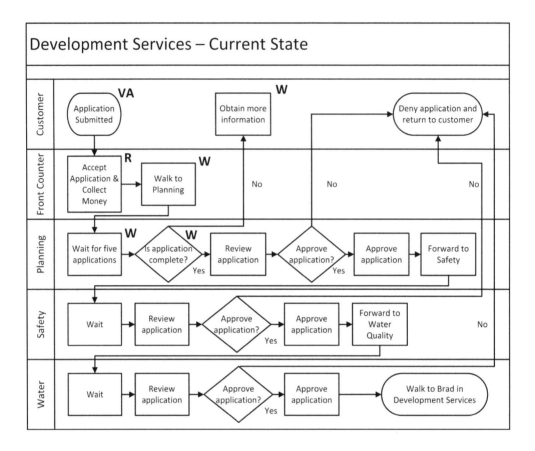

"Cindy," Karen said, "you are in Planning. Go ahead and identify the rest of the steps in your swim lane."

"I'll give it a shot," Cindy said. "The process steps of 'review application' and 'approve application' are both 'Value Added' steps as we are comparing the application to our zoning codes. The decision step of 'approve application?' is a 'Required' step, the 'deny application' is a 'Value Added' step as we made a determination on the application, and the 'forward to safety' is a 'Waste' step."

"Good job," Karen said.

Adam raised his hand and said, "If the file was already at Safety, there wouldn't be a need to forward it to us. Why are we waiting for Planning to review the file before Safety gets it?"

"Yes, each department is waiting for the other to finish," Brad said. "That certainly adds a lot of time."

"Why don't we all review the same file at the same time?" Keisha asked.

"You certainly could," Karen said. "Let's add that to the Action List and discuss at a later time." Karen added to the list.

Action Items
1) Look into eliminating batching applications at Planning
2) Develop one universal application for all five divisions
3) Eliminate the approval step at Environmental Health
4) Train the front counter person to check if the application is complete at the front counter
5) All five divisions review the file at the same time

"Let me update our map," Karen said.

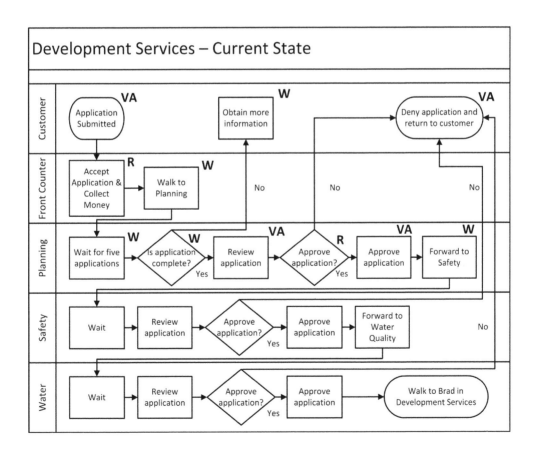

"Adam," Karen said, "you're in Safety, why don't you identify the steps in your swim lane."

"The 'wait' step is obviously a 'Waste' step," Adam said. "The process steps of 'review application' and 'approve application' are 'Value Added' steps, the decision step of 'approve application?' is a 'Required' step, the 'deny application' is 'Value Added', and 'forward to water quality' is a 'Waste' step.

"I agree and let me add those indications to the process map," Karen said.

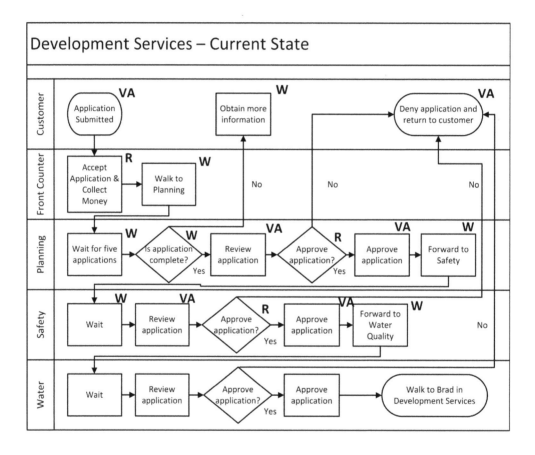

"Patel," Karen said, "would the steps in your swim lane be the same?"

"Let me look," Patel said. "I would agree. And the last step of 'walk to Brad' is a 'Waste' step."

"Let me update our map," Karen said.

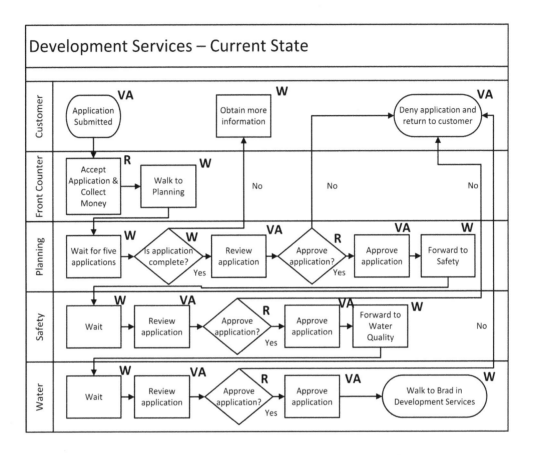

"When I look at the process map," Tim said, "I notice that we don't have one single point of contact when we're interacting with the customer. Each division does it separately. That seems to be a waste of extra-processing."

"I'd agree," Patel said.

"Let's add that problem to the Action List," Cindy said.

"Will do," Karen said and added it to the list.

Action Items
1) Look into eliminating batching applications at Planning
2) Develop one universal application for all five divisions
3) Eliminate the approval step at Environmental Health
4) Train the front counter person to check if the application is complete at the front counter
5) All five divisions review the file at the same time
6) Have one single point of contact with the customer

"Tim and Keisha," Karen said, "your process flows are both very similar. Why don't you get together and study your process maps. Identify the 'Value Added', 'Required', and 'Waste' steps. The rest of us can stand up and stretch our legs."

* * *

"I think we have our response," Keisha said. "By comparing our two maps with the previous one for Planning, Safety, and Water, we have very similar classification of the steps. For example, the 'application submitted', 'review application', and 'deny application' are all 'Value Added'. All of these steps changed the permit application in either form or function."

"I agree," Tim said. "The decision steps are 'Required'. And the 'waiting' and 'walking' are all 'Waste' steps."

"And the steps to obtain my supervisor's signature," Keisha said, "are all 'Waste' steps since she automatically signs every application."

"Thanks Keisha and Tim," Karen said. "Let me add your process step classifications to the maps."

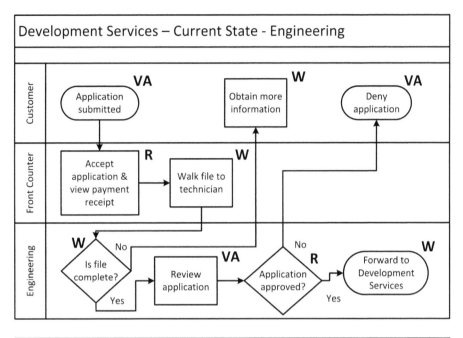

Development Services – Current State - Engineering

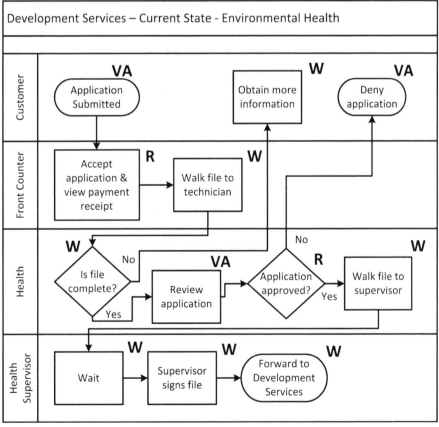

Development Services – Current State - Environmental Health

"Do these look correct?" Karen asked.

Tim and Keisha nodded in agreement.

"Our final map," Karen said, "is where Brad collects the responses from the five divisions and makes a determination if the permit should be issued or denied."

"Here you go," Brad said. "I already wrote down my responses." Brad handed Karen the marked up process flow map and Karen added his responses to the white board.

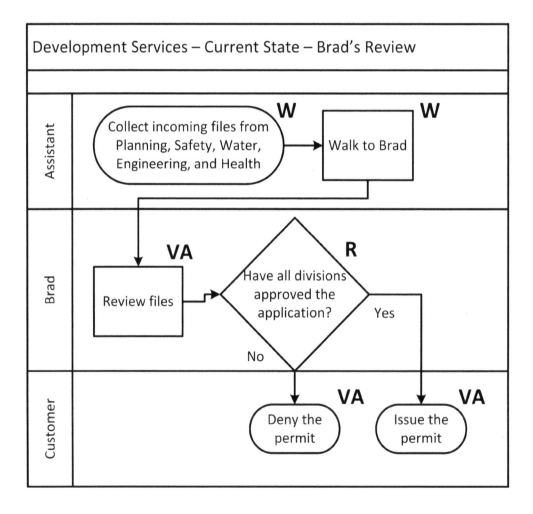

"Everyone take a look and see if you agree," Karen said.

"They look correct to me," Tim said. "The 'Value Added' steps are 'reviewing the file' and then 'issuing or denying the permit'. All of these changed the form or function of the application and it was something that the customer wanted us to do."

"Let's look back at all four maps," Karen said, "and count how many steps it took for one permit to be issued."

"I come up with forty-eight steps," Tim said.

"That seems like a lot of steps just to issue one permit," Patel said. "And how many permits do we issue every year."

"About 4,000," Brad said.

"Wow," Keisha said. "When you multiply the number of steps to issue one permit by the number of permits we issue every year, it comes out to 192,000 steps!"

"No wonder we can't keep up," Cindy said.

"See what happens when you analyze a process," Karen said.

"I just did a quick count of the 'Waste' steps," Adam said. "I came up with twenty-two out of the forty-eight steps are pure waste. That's almost 50% of our process."

"And if you multiply the 'Waste' steps by the number of permits we issue each year," Keisha said, "I come up with 88,000 individual steps that add no value whatsoever."

Tim sighed, "I feel tired already."

"You did a great job today," Karen said. "You analyzed the process and saw how you are wasting almost 50% of your time to issue permits."

Karen turned toward Tim, "Remember earlier you suggested that we make the files electronic and by-pass this Analysis phase?"

"I do," Tim said. "And I must admit that if we followed that suggestion, we would have missed out on a lot of other 'Waste' steps."

"What were some of those?" Karen asked.

"We would have missed the redundant approval step by my supervisor," Keisha said.

"And not having all five divisions review the file simultaneously," Brad said.

"And not batching the application at Planning," Cindy said.

"Don't forget about having one application instead of three," Patel said.

"As you can see," Karen said, "without a thorough analysis of the process, we would have missed these 'Waste' steps."

"The result would have been sub-optimal," Tim said. "Just as you said."

"And speaking of 'Waste'," Cindy said, "I've been keeping a list of the examples of the eight wastes that we found at Development Service. Here is what I came up with." Cindy showed her list to the group.

Waste	Example at Development Services
Defects	Missing information on the application due to three different applications
Over-Production	Customer filling out three applications
Waiting	Sequential review by the five divisions, waiting for supervisor approval
Non-Utilized People	Front-counter person not properly trained
Transportation	Walking files from division to division
Inventory	Batching files
Motion	Walking back to your workstation after dropping off the file
Extra-Processing	All five divisions contacting the customer

The group was silent for a moment and read the list.

"Wow, Cindy," Brad said, "this is great. It really summarizes what we've been doing here the past couple of weeks."

"I agree," Karen said. "Good job."

"Karen, thank you so much for leading us over these past couple of weeks," Tim said. "This has really opened my eyes on how we do things around here."

"My pleasure," Karen said. "Give yourselves a round of applause."

The group high-fived and the meeting came to an end.

Chapter 22

Carl knocked on Sam's office door frame and waited.

"Hi Carl," Sam said. He waved Carl into his office, over to the oval table and closed the door. "Have a seat."

"Thanks again for visiting with the Council Members," Sam said. "Did you gain any insight?"

"I was able to sit down for some casual conversations with Trisha and the other Council Members," Carl said. "I must say that they all have the greatest respect for you. They like your personality, friendly disposition, and smile. And everyone acknowledged your many years of service to the City of Neal and were very grateful."

"Go on," Sam said. "How are they feeling about my upcoming performance review?"

"We did talk about that," Carl said, "and this is where things aren't as upbeat . . . everyone I talked with felt that things are not going well with the city. Nearly everyone brought up complaints from citizens in their district. Council Member Hernandez even had a few angry e-mails to show me. And some of the business leaders are not so happy either."

Sam lowered his head and took a deep breath. "I see."

"Sam, I defended you, I really did," Carl said. "I talked about how we haven't laid-off anyone in over three years, how we're not filling positions when people leave voluntarily, and how we're still managing to keep up with basic services."

"Did you have a chance to meet with Mayor Denim?" Sam asked.

"Not yet," Carl said. "He was travelling for most of this past week."

"What else can you tell me about your meetings?" Sam asked.

"The mood is just not good," Carl said. "Several Council Members brought up that negative newspaper article from a few weeks back."

"That may be the final nail in my coffin," Sam said. "I keep hearing rumors about how the Council is ready to change leadership. By the way, did you ever get in touch with that newspaper reporter that wrote the article?"

"You know how the press is," Carl said. "He never did get back to me. But I'll keep trying."

Standing up Sam felt his chest tighten again. He walked from the oval conference table and sat down in his desk chair and looked around his office.

"Lots of memories here Carl," Sam said. "All of these certificates, plaques, and awards mean something to me. And yet they all may mean nothing in a few weeks." Sam stared out the window and saw nearly bare trees.

"Carl, what do you think I should do?"

"Sam, I hate to say this, but have you ever thought of going into early retirement? I mean that would be a good way to save face and not have to deal with all of these issues here at the city."

"I have," Sam said, "but I'm not the quitting type." Sam clenched his fist and slammed it onto his desk. "Dammit, I'll sit in my office until they force me to go." The room was silent for a few moments. Sam wiped sweat from his brow.

"What's happening with Karen and the DMAIC team?" Sam asked.

"Not such good news there either," Carl said. "There's been some in-fighting amongst the team members and very little progress. Some employees are resisting change. And there's lots of griping about what the team is trying to do."

"Yeah," Sam said. "Larry came into my office the other day and bitched."

"Sam," Carl said, "I don't think this Lean thing is going to work for us here. I wouldn't bring that effort up during your performance review."

"Not a lot of options left," Sam said staring straight ahead. "One last option is to meet with Mayor Denim and get his thoughts."

Sam stood. "Carl, thanks again for your help—on the way out, can you have Patty set up a meeting between me and the mayor as soon as possible."

"Will do," Carl said. "Hang in there buddy. I'm here for you."

"Thanks," Sam said and Carl left his office. Patty was on the phone. Carl sat in one of the reception chairs waiting for her to finish the call. After a few minutes Patty was done with the call.

"Patty, Sam asked me to have you set up a meeting between him and Mayor Denim as soon as their schedules allow."

"Will do," Patty said and Carl left to go to another meeting.

Patty opened up the calendars for Sam and Mayor Denim on the computer and found a time on Friday when they could meet. Picking up her note pad, Patty walked into Sam's office and said, "Sam, there is an open time to meet with the mayor on ..."

She stopped in her tracks. Sam was hunched over his desk. "Sam, Sam, SAM!" she yelled, rushed over and shook Sam's shoulder. No response. She shook harder. Nothing. "Oh my God!" she said. "SAM CAN YOU HEAR ME!"

She picked up Sam's phone and dialed 911.

"911 what is your emergency?"

"This is Patty Douglas in the City Manager's office in the Neal City Hall on Surrey Road. Send an ambulance over right now. I think Sam's had a heart attack."

END OF PART 2

* * *

Part 3

A light snow was falling on Wednesday morning. The roads were wet, but driving conditions not bad. Karen hoped that the weather didn't cause any problems for the DMAIC team members. Especially as they were meeting in a conference room at a local hotel. Karen parked and hurried through the snowflakes to the lobby. A front desk clerk greeted her.

"Hello," Karen said, "Can you tell me where the City of Neal meeting room is?"

"They're in the Cave Creek room, right down this corridor."

"Thanks," Karen said and walked toward the meeting room. She entered and found Keisha, Brad, Adam, Cindy, Patel and Tim all sitting at the tables.

"Good morning everyone," Karen said. "I hope that the drive in today was OK."

"No problem," Adam said.

"Luckily, the snow isn't sticking to the roads," Brad said.

"So why are we meeting off-site?" Cindy asked.

"Creativity," Karen said as she took off her coat and sat down. "As we move into the Improve phase, we need to create a 'future state' of our process. To do that, we need to rid ourselves of conventional thinking. And to encourage creative thinking, I wanted to physically remove us from our familiar surroundings. No longer can we accept the answer of 'this is way we have always done things around here'. We need to be creative and original in our thinking."

"Sounds good," Adam said. "I like being more casually dressed and away from the office."

Karen pointed to the flip charts and said, "Just like I requested, I see that the hotel brought in the portable white boards and flip charts. Today we will be building a new process flow for Development Services and will need lots of room to post our ideas."

"How do we start?" Cindy asked.

"Let's first look at the four process maps we developed at our last meeting and list the 'Value Added' and the 'Required' steps. I made copies of the maps we produced." Karen passed out paper copies of the maps. "Tim, can you identify the 'Value Added' step?"

"By looking at the maps," Tim said, "the 'Value Added' steps include the customer submitting the application, the five divisions reviewing the application, and accepting or rejecting the application."

"Boy, only four different types of value added steps," Brad said. "That's not many considering that we take forty five steps to issue a permit."

"However, there are five divisions all doing the same review," Tim said. "So the total number of 'Value Added' steps is a bit higher. But as you can see, the only real value we add is to accept the application, review it, and make a final determination on it."

"How about the 'Required' steps?" Karen asked. "How many of these steps did we identify?"

"Here's what I came up with," Keisha said. "The first 'Required' step is the process step when we accept the application and collect money. And the second 'Required' step is a decision step to approve the application. Each one of our five divisions has these two steps."

"Right," Karen said. "Both of these steps don't add any value but they are required in order to review the application. These four 'Value Added' steps and two 'Required' steps can be our starting point for building a 'future state' map. And what's our goal with the 'Required' steps?"

"Minimize them," Patel said. "They may be required, but we should try and minimize them as much as possible."

"And what is our goal with the 'Waste' steps?" Karen asked. "Eliminate them!" Tim, Brad, and Keisha said in unison.

"Good," Karen said with a smile. "I like the enthusiasm. Let me add these steps on the white board."

Value Added Steps	Required Steps
Customer submits the application	Accept the application and collect money
Review the application	Approve the application?
Reject the application	
Accept the application	

"Another item to consider," Karen said, "is the actual processing time that each division spends on the application. Here's the list of time we developed at a previous meeting." Karen passed out the list of processing and lead times.

Department	Lead Time	Processing Time
Engineering	7 days	6 hours
Environmental Health	14 days	2 hours
Planning	8 days	2 hours
Water Quality	11 days	7 hours
Safety	12 days	5 hours
TOTAL	**52 days**	**22 hours**

"What's the total processing time for all five divisions?" Karen asked.

"Adding them up comes to twenty-two hours," Patel said.

"Good," Karen said. "That passes the first test which is: Can we meet the goal of reviewing and issuing a house renovation permit within the stated fifteen business days? And I would say that the answer is yes."

"Let's also take a look," Karen said, "at our action item list that we developed at our last meeting. Let me write it out on the white board."

Action Items
1) Look into eliminating batching applications at Planning
2) Develop one universal application for all five divisions
3) Eliminate the approval step at Environmental Health
4) Train the front counter person to check if the application is complete at the front counter
5) All five divisions review the file at the same time
6) Have one single point of contact with the customer

"To create a 'future state'," Karen said, "we need to do some brain storming. Who's been involved with brain storming in the past?"

Tim, Patel, and Cindy all raised their hands.

"What are some of the ground rules when brainstorming?" Karen asked.

"No criticism of ideas," Cindy said.

"Think outside of the box," Tim said.

"Build on other people's ideas," Patel said.

"Good answers," Karen said. "The idea of brainstorming is to generate as many ideas as possible to overcome our obstacles. Don't worry if the idea is feasible or not or if your supervisor would accept it or not."

"When I did brainstorming," Tim said, "I had fun with adding to an existing idea. I like being creative."

"To kick-start our brainstorming," Karen said, "let me pass out the eight wastes that we identified previously." Karen passed out the list.

Waste	Example at Development Services
Defects	Missing information on the application due to three different applications
Over-Production	Customer filling out three applications
Waiting	Sequential review by the five divisions, waiting for supervisor approval
Non-Utilized People	Front-counter person not properly trained
Transportation	Walking files from division to division
Inventory	Batching files
Motion	Walking back to your workstation after dropping off the file
Extra-Processing	All five divisions contacting the customer

"OK, let's do a round-robin approach and go around the table and shout out an idea. I'll write it on the white board. If you are out of ideas, say 'pass' and the next person goes. If you say 'pass' you can always join in if another idea comes to mind. If it helps, refer to the list of action items and the list of the eight wastes. These are some of the problems that we're trying to overcome."

"Tim," Karen said, "you are sitting on the left hand side, let's start with you."

"Looking at the 'action item' and the 'eight wastes' list, I would say one universal application. This would minimize some defects and also eliminate the waste of over-production for the customer."

Karen wrote the suggestion on the board.

Brainstorming Ideas
1) One universal application

"Patel, your turn," Karen said.

"Have all five divisions review the file at the same time," Patel said. "That would eliminate much, but not all, of the waste of waiting." Karen wrote that one the white board.

Brainstorming Ideas
1) One universal application
2) All five divisions review the file simultaneously

"Cindy?" Karen asked.

"What if we co-located the five divisions in one building to eliminate the customer from driving to three locations?"

"Oh, I like that," Brad said.

"Tim?" Karen asked.

"Let's eliminate the waste of walking the files by sending them electronically to each division?"

Brainstorming Ideas
1) One universal application
2) All five divisions review the file simultaneously
3) Co-locate the five divisions in one building
4) Send files electronically

"Adam?" Karen asked.

"No custom home applications," Adam said. "They just seem to take so long to review."

The group chuckled in agreement.

"As I said, no criticism," Karen said. "On the list it goes. Tim, continue please."

"No batching files," Tim said.

"How about a totally electronic submission and review," Brad said. "This would eliminate the customer from having to drive to our office completely."

"Good," Karen said.

"Limit applications to five a day," Patel said.

The group laughed.

"Train the front counter person to look for missing information right from the start," Cindy said. "This would eliminate the waste of a non-utilized person."

"What else, any other ideas?" Karen asked.

"Pass," Tim said.

"Same for me," Patel said.

"What about giving authority to the reviewers to approve the application," Cindy said.

"That would eliminate me always waiting for my supervisor's signature," Keisha said.

"Good thought," Karen said. "Any other ideas?"

The group was silent and nodded their heads that they were out of ideas.

"OK, let's look at our 'brainstorming' list," Karen said.

Brainstorming Ideas
1) One universal application
2) All five divisions review the file simultaneously
3) Co-locate the five divisions in one building
4) Send files electronically
5) No custom home applications
6) No batching files
7) Electronic submission and review
8) Limit applications to five per day
9) Train the front counter person to look for missing information
10) Allow reviewers, and not supervisors, to approve the application

"As you can see," Karen said, "the items from the 'action item' list are also on the 'brainstorming' list. And many of your ideas overcame the waste problems we identified."

"But there are also some new ideas on the brainstorming list," Patel said, "that didn't come up in the value stream mapping exercise."

"That's the value of doing both," Karen said. "We now have a very complete list to look at and see what we can implement. Let's take a break. When we come back, we'll start building a 'future state' process flow map for Development Services."

The group stood up and left the conference room.

Chapter 24

Laura heard a knock at her front door. She opened the door, to see Robert from IT. "Hi Robert," she said. "Come on in."

"Thanks Laura," Robert said. "How's Sam doing?" They walked into the kitchen.

"Just sitting in bed and resting," Laura said. "But he certainly isn't a very good patient."

"What do you mean?" Robert asked.

"The doctor told him to stay off of his feet and rest," Laura said. "All he wants to do is wander around the house and try and fix something. Today I finally got him to stay in bed, but yesterday, he was ready to install a new sink garbage disposal!"

Robert smiled. "He does enjoy his home improvement projects. And how are *you* holding out Laura?"

"Overall pretty good," Laura said. "I'm getting more relaxed every day. I talked with my supervisor at the real estate office and he's giving me a leave of absence and letting me take as much time as I need to stay home with Sam."

"That's good. I heard that Sam's prognosis is promising," Robert said.

"The doctor said that it was a minor heart attack," Laura said, "with no long term damage. He needs to rest and rebuild his strength, but otherwise, things are as good as can be hoped for."

"That's great news," Robert said.

"The doctor said that it really helped that Sam was trim and in good physical shape," Laura said. "The heart attack was caused by all of the stress that Sam is under at work. So I'm trying to shield him from talking about work much."

"Sounds good," Robert said. "Can I see him now?"

"Of course," Laura said. Robert and Laura walked upstairs to the master bedroom. Sam was reading a newspaper.

"Honey, you have a visitor," Laura said.

"Robert!" Sam said with a big smile. "It's so good to see you. Thanks for coming over."

"No problem buddy," Robert said. "How are you feeling?"

"Great," Sam said. "And eager to get up and move around."

"I heard you wanted to install a new sink disposal yesterday," Robert joked.

"Yes, but Laura wouldn't let me," Sam said. "Now Robert, tell Laura that installing the disposal is easy. I can certainly do it now."

"Sam," Laura said sternly, "we went over this yesterday. And we agreed to no physical activity until Dr. Palmer says it's OK."

"I know, I know," Sam muttered.

"Let me leave you two guys alone," Laura said. "Robert, can I offer you anything to drink?"

"No, I'm fine, thanks Laura," Robert said.

Laura left the room and went downstairs.

"So are you doing OK?" Robert asked.

"Yes, I feel fine," Sam said. "Just a little bored. I hate sitting all day. I'd rather be at work or working on the rental house."

"Oh, I got some good news about the rental," Robert said. "The boys and I went over this past weekend and we finished installing the kitchen cabinets."

"Robert, thank you so much," Sam said.

"Oh no problem," Robert said. "It was great for my boys to gain some experience with house projects. My youngest really seems to like it, but my oldest just goes along because he has to."

"We've all got different interests," Sam said. "I'll have to get your boys some gift cards to thank them."

"Not necessary," Robert said. "But I'm sure that they would appreciate it."

"So how's the IT department these days?" Sam asked.

"Not bad," Robert said. "We just finished installing the new software for Public Works and next week we start on upgrading the HR training program."

"Glad to hear that things are going good," Sam said.

"I also wanted to tell you," Robert said, "how excited Karen is to be working on the DMAIC team. Whenever I see her around the office, she seems so full of energy. She can't wait to tell me about the progress the team is making."

"Really?" Sam asked. "I heard that the project was stalled."

"Not according to Karen," Robert said. "She told me how they mapped out the existing process and how they found all this waste in the process. I heard they also listed a bunch of action items to help shorten the flow even further."

"How long ago was this?" Sam asked.

"Just yesterday," Robert said, "she told me how the team was preparing to map out the future state. I really like Karen's style; she's a good team leader."

"Yea, I do too," Sam said. "What you just said seems to contradict with what I heard."

"Maybe you can give Karen a call," Robert said, "and get the latest update from her."

Sam stared into space. "I think I'll do that."

"I should get back to the office," Robert said. "Let me know if there is anything that I can do for you Sam."

"No, no Robert," Sam said. "You've done enough already. More than you probably know. Thanks again for coming to see me."

"Catch you later, pal."

Chapter 25

"Thanks for buying us donuts at the coffee shop," Cindy said as the group returned to the Cave Creek room at the hotel.

"No problem," Karen said. "This will go on my expense report. Today is a work day."

"And it's certainly refreshing to be away from the office," Brad said.

"It's all part of building an innovative atmosphere," Karen said. "Let's look again at the 'brainstorming' list we created this morning. Does anyone have anything to add?"

"I had a thought," Tim said. "What if the front counter person acts as the main point of contact for the customer from start to finish?"

"I like that," Cindy said. "That would keep communication consistent with the customer."

"The front counter person," Brad said, "can also be responsible for ensuring that the permit gets responded to within fifteen days."

"Good," Karen said. "In effect, you are making this person a one-stop shop for the customer."

"Good idea," Brad said. "Let's add that to the list."

Karen added to the list on the white board.

Brainstorming Ideas
1) One universal application
2) All five divisions review the file simultaneously
3) Co-locate the five divisions in one building
4) Send files electronically
5) No custom home applications
6) No batching files
7) Electronic submission and review
8) Limit applications to five per day
9) Train the front counter person to look for missing information
10) Allow reviewers, and not supervisors, to approve the application
11) The font-counter person be the one point of contact with the customer

"Now we need to connect-the-dots," Karen said. "We have identified the value added and the required steps and we also have a list of creative ideas. Our goal for the rest of today is to draw a future state map with as few steps as possible. The first question we need to tackle is; do we still need seven swim lanes for the future state map? The lanes are 'customer', 'front desk', 'planning', 'safety', 'water quality', 'engineering', and 'health'.

"It seems like we need all seven," Brad said. "Even if we co-locate the five divisions under one roof, we still have five divisions that need to approve the permit application."

"What does everyone else think?" Karen asked.

"I would agree," Cindy said. The others nodded.

"Then let's keep the swim lanes as they are," Karen said.

Karen drew a blank process flow map on the board.

Development Services – Future State		
Customer		
Front Counter		
Planning		
Safety		
Water		
Engineering		
Health		

"We now need to place the 'Value Added' steps on the map," Karen said.

"Since every division ultimately has to review the application," Patel said, "I would put this step in each of our lanes."

Karen added these steps to the map.

Development Services – Future State	

Customer	
Front Counter	
Planning	Planning review
Safety	Safety review
Water	Water review
Engineering	Engineering review
Health	Health review

"The other 'Value Added' steps are connected with the client," Keisha said. "We should add 'submit application', 'approve permit', and 'deny permit' to the customer's swim lane."

"Will do," Karen said and added them to the map.

Development Services – Future State

"Also," Patel said, "let's have the front counter person review the file for completeness right when they initially meet with the customer. This will cut down the time between when the customer submits the application and when the technicians review it,"

"I like that," Tim said. "And as we mentioned this morning, we'll need to train the front counter person to look for problems."

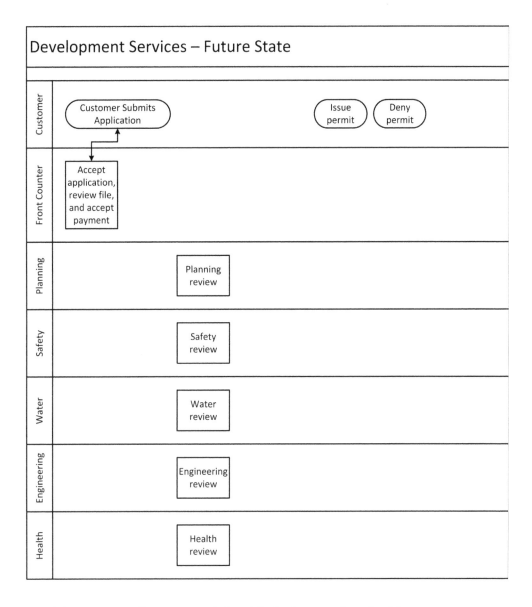

"If you notice," Karen said, "I added a line with a double arrow connecting the front counter to the customer. This indicates that the front counter person is reviewing the application with the customer and obtaining more information if needed."

"That will eliminate," Adam said, "the delay of having one of the technicians review the file for completeness *after* the customer has left the building."

"What other ideas can we use," Karen said, "to connect the value added steps in the shortest possible manner."

"We talked about routing the application electronically," Tim said. "This would eliminate all of the waste of 'transportation' of carrying the file to the next division and the waste of 'motion' of returning to your desk."

"What does everyone think?" Karen asked. "How can we depict this step?"

"Right after the front counter person accepts the application," Keisha said, "put a process step of 'forward electronic file to five divisions'. Then draw lines from this process step to the five 'review' steps by each department.

"Like this?" Karen asked.

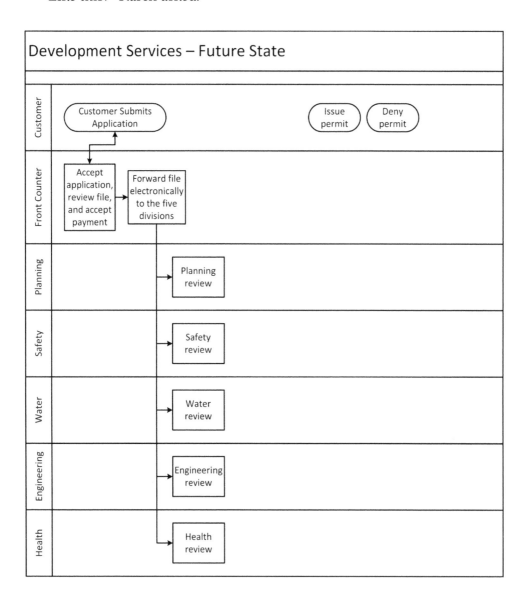

"Yes," Keisha said. "That looks good."

"Once each division has reviewed the application," Adam said, "they can forward it to Brad electronically."

"Then I'll do a review of the five files," Brad said. "And the end result will either be to issue the permit, deny the permit, or request additional information from the client."

"How does this look?" Karen asked.

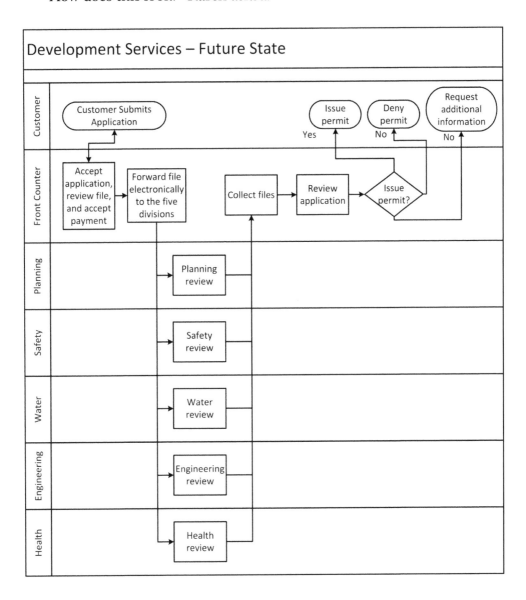

"It looks good to me," Keisha said.

"Now let's do a quick analysis of our 'future state' map," Karen said. "What is the total number of steps in our 'future state'?" Karen asked.

"I count fourteen steps," Keisha said.

"That's a lot lower," Brad said, "than the forty-five steps we identified in the 'current state'."

"And what's the number of 'Value Added', 'Required', and 'Waste' steps?" Karen asked.

"As we previously identified," Patel said, "the 'Value Added' steps are the customer submitting the application, the five division reviews, and issuing or denying the permit. However, we can now classify the front counter person reviewing the application with the customer as a 'Value Added' step."

"That's correct," Karen said. "Since there is a review of the application while the customer is there, this step can be considered 'Value Added' as the customer wants us to do it."

Karen added to the process flow.

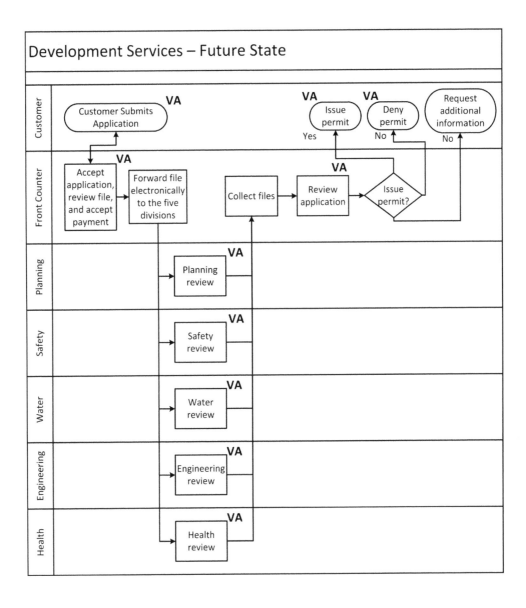

"Forwarding and collecting the five applications are 'Waste' steps," Tim said. "They don't add any value. And issuing the permit and requesting additional information are both 'Required' steps."

Karen added to the process flow.

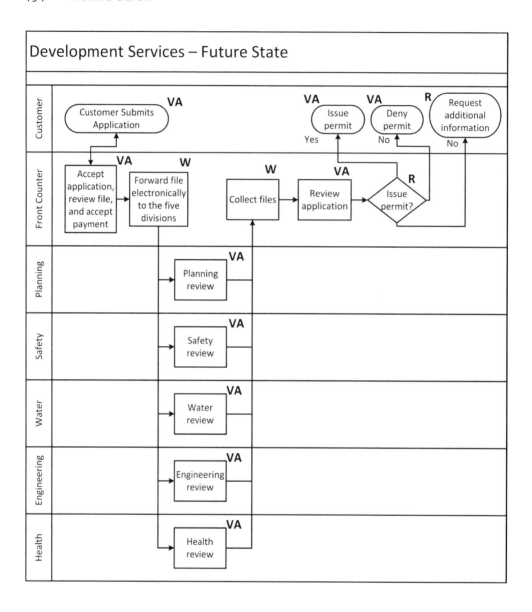

Development Services – Future State

"Here's my count," Patel said. "I list ten 'Value Added' steps, two 'Required' steps, and two 'Waste' steps."

"That a good distribution," Karen said. "The 'future state' process flow should contain predominately 'Value Added' steps with a minimal amount of 'Required' and 'Waste' steps."

"The process flow looks so much cleaner," Adam said.

"And we condensed four separate process flows into one," Cindy said.

"You did a great job creating this new flow," Karen said. "This 'future state' process map is our goal for Development Services. We will meet again in a few days back at the City of Neal offices. There, we need to come up with a plan to implement this new future state. We'll start with a pilot test to see if it gives us the results we're looking for. Great job everyone."

The team applauded.

"We're getting close to the lunch hour," Karen said. "What if we have lunch at the hotel's restaurant?"

"Are you buying?" Patel asked.

"Oh course," Karen said.

"Then I'm hungry," Patel said. "Let's go."

Tim grinned. "You're always hungry."

The group headed out the door.

Chapter 26

The next day, Karen was sitting at her desk, updating the latest process flow map on her computer. The phone rang.

"Hello, this is Karen."

"Hi Karen, its Sam."

"Sam, so good to hear from you, how are you feeling?"

"Actually, pretty good," Sam said. "Laura has been diligent on having me rest and I'm feeling stronger every day."

"That's wonderful," Karen said.

"Although I will say," Sam said, "that I am getting a bit bored being home all day long."

"Any thoughts on when you'll return to work?" Karen asked.

"I'm seeing Dr. Palmer next week," Sam said. "We'll see what he advises."

"We all miss you around here," Karen said. "I hope you make it back to work soon."

"Me too," Sam said. "How are things going for you Karen? How's the DMAIC project coming along?"

"We're making great progress," Karen said. "The group is so wonderful to work with; everyone comes to the meetings well prepared and full of ideas."

"So you *are* making progress?" Sam asked.

"Yes," Karen said. "We defined the problem as 'sixty days is too long to issue permits' and set the new goal at fifteen days. We measured the lead and processing times for each division. We process-flow mapped the current process and came up with a long list of areas to improve. We created a future state process flow and will test it out with a pilot program. I really think that we can make the goal of fifteen days to issue a permit."

"That's great to hear," Sam said. "No in-fighting between the group members?"

"Not in the least," Karen said. "Everyone really supports and encourages each other."

"That's—uh, thanks—good to hear," Sam said. "What's next for the group?"

"We're starting the pilot project," Karen said. "We want to test out the new process flow on a small scale to see if we get the efficiency we want."

"How soon before you know?" Sam asked.

"Within the next two to three weeks," Karen said.

"Karen, I have my performance evaluation coming up in three weeks," Sam said. "It certainly would be nice to get some tangible results before the review."

"Knowing that," Karen said, "I'll push up the implementation schedule and finish the pilot run as soon as possible."

"Thanks Karen," Sam said. "I appreciate it."

"No problem," Karen said. "Thanks for letting me and the group work on this project."

"Oh, one more thing," Sam said. "Is Carl aware of your effort?"

"Yes," Karen said. "I always type up my notes after each DMAIC team meeting and forward them to Carl. I've also met with him a few times in person and I've given him all of the details on our progress."

"That's . . . that's good to know," Sam said.

"Take care Sam," Karen said. "Hope to see you in the office soon. Goodbye."

Sam hung up the phone and sat in silence for a few moments. He picked up the phone and called Robert in IT.

"Robert, this is Sam. Are you alone in your office? Good. I need you to do some investigation for me. Here's what I need ..."

Chapter 27

A few days later, Karen entered the DMAIC conference room at the City of Neal offices. She saw everyone there except Cindy. "Good morning everyone, how are you today?"

"Just fine," Tim said.

"Eager to try out the new process flow," Brad said.

"Cindy is out sick today," Keisha said.

"I'm sorry," Karen said. "I hope she feels better soon."

"I hope so too," Keisha said.

"Today," Karen said, "we'll implement a pilot program for our new proposed flow for Development Services."

"Why is this necessary?" Tim asked.

"Even though we think that the new flow will work," Karen said, "we need to test it out to see if we get the results we want. It's also a good idea to test out the concepts while investing the minimal amount of money. If it looks like we're getting the results we wanted, then we can look into investing additional time and money to make this a permanent change."

"How long should we test out the new flow?" Patel asked.

"Long enough to see tangible results," Karen said. "I think that after two weeks, we'll know if the new process is working or not. And besides, sometimes during a pilot test you'll come up with a better idea or we'll find a new problem we didn't think about before. What we need to do at this point is define the tasks needed to start a pilot program and then assign a person responsible for it."

"Do we need to run a parallel program," Brad said, "where we run both the existing and the pilot program at the same time?"

"Yes," Karen said, "it's good practice to run a pilot program concurrently alongside the existing process. For our purposes, we can take a sample of permit applications and route them through the new flow."

"What if we took ever other application submitted," Keisha said, "and ran it through the new process."

"I like that," Brad said. "This would give us a comparison for permits running through both processes."

"Let's start the list of items to implement," Karen said, "and then list the person responsible."

"The first thing we need to do," Brad said, "is to make the application electronic and eliminate the paper file. I can take on *part* of this task by scanning the drawings and supplemental paperwork submitted by the customer. But what I will need help with is the electronic application."

"I can take that one," Patel said. "I've done electronic applications in the past."

"Great," Karen said. "Patel, why don't you produce a new electronic application that contains the information contained in the three existing applications. How long will it take you to do this?"

"I'll have it done by end-of-day tomorrow," Patel said.

"Fantastic," Brad said.

"Let me start an implementation list on the white board," Karen said, "and include the person responsible."

Pilot Run Task List	
Task	Responsible Person
Combine the three applications and create one electronic application	Patel
Set up scanner for drawings and other paperwork	Brad

"What other tasks do we have?" Karen asked.

"Let's put a representative," Keisha said, "from Engineering and Environmental Health in the Development Services building for these two weeks. Even though we'll be e-mailing the files to each other, it would help if we were all physically close to each other if questions came up."

"Good idea," Karen said.

"I'll talk with my supervisor," Tim said, "and see if I can sit at Development Services for these two weeks."

"Same with me," Keisha said. "It would either be me or one of our technicians who would sit at Development Services. I'll check with my supervisor and let the group know."

Karen added to the list.

Pilot Run Task List	
Task	Responsible Person
Combine the three applications and create one electronic application	Patel
Set up scanner for drawings and other paperwork	Brad
Place an Engineering representative at Development Services	Tim
Place an Environmental Health representative at Development Services	Keisha

"What about the front counter person?" Keisha asked. "Any suggestions on who we could use for this two week test?"

"I'll volunteer to do that," Brad said. "I probably have the most knowledge of how the five different divisions operate. And if I have any questions, I know who to contact."

"Does that sound OK to the group?" Karen asked.

"Thanks for volunteering," Tim said. "Watch out what you ask for."

Brad smiled and said, "I know, but this is something that I have been thinking of doing for some while now. And besides, the front counter experience will give me an idea on how to train future front counter attendants."

"Let's review," Karen said. "We have Patel creating an electronic application that combines the existing three. We have Brad scanning the supplemental documents that will travel with the application. We have Brad working the front counter, and we will investigate having Tim and Keisha stationed at Development Services for our two week pilot program. What else, anything else that we are missing?"

"I talked with my supervisor at Environmental Health," Keisha said, "and she gave me guidelines on what I can approve without her review. So unless something unusual comes up during the pilot run, I will have approval authority."

"That's great," Karen said. "Thanks for checking into that. Let me add that to the list." Karen added to the list.

Pilot Run Task List	
Task	Responsible Person
Combine the three applications and create one electronic application	Patel
Set up scanner for drawings and other paperwork	Brad
Place an Engineering representative at Development Services	Tim
Place an Environmental Health representative at Development Services	Keisha
Front counter person	Brad
No requirement for Environmental Health supervisor approval	Keisha

"What else are we missing," Karen said, "in order to run this pilot program?"

"What about the performance metrics?" Keisha asked. "How will we know if the new process is working or not?"

"Good point," Karen said. "Any ideas on tracking our performance but still keeping things simple?"

"How about this idea," Brad said. "I'll be working the front counter and e-mailing the application to everyone. That will be our reference start time. I'll then compare it to the date when I receive everyone's comments back and then issue or deny the permit."

"That sounds pretty simple," Patel said. "The e-mails to and from Brad will be date stamped and Brad can easily track the time."

"Along with the time," Tim said, "can I suggest that we also document the type of permit we are dealing with? Such as whether it was an existing home renovation, a new home construction, or a business permit."

"I like that idea," Karen said. "When Brad is tabulating the time, he can also list the type of permit being issued. Good idea Tim."

"Thanks," Tim said.

Karen added to the list.

Pilot Run Task List	
Task	Responsible Person
Combine the three applications and create one electronic application	Patel
Set up scanner for drawings and other paperwork	Brad
Place an Engineering representative at Development Services	Tim
Place an Environmental Health representative at Development Services	Keisha
Front counter person	Brad
No requirement for Environmental Health supervisor approval	Keisha
Track performance metrics	Brad

"Anything else we should be concerned with?" Karen asked.

"As you said," Adam said, "there will probably be things we haven't thought about and need to deal with during the pilot program, but this is a great start."

"Fantastic," Karen said. "Let's start the pilot program on Monday."

"Oh, this is so exciting," Patel said.

"I agree," Brad said

The meeting came to an end.

Chapter 28

"Honey, I'll get the door," Laura said as she walked to the front door of their house and opened it. She saw Carl standing there.

"Hi Carl, good to see you," Laura said. "Come on in."

"Thanks Laura," Carl said. "How are you doing this lovely day?"

"Oh just fine, and you?"

"Busy," Carl said. "With Sam gone these past several weeks, I've been trying to keep the ship afloat."

"I'm sure that you're doing a wonderful job," Laura said. "And besides, Sam met with Dr. Palmer and it looks like he can go back to work soon, at least on a limited basis."

"That's great to hear," Carl said. "We all miss him at the office. Sam called me yesterday and asked me to come over to your house for a meeting. I guess your house is now the de facto City Manager's office."

"I've gotten used to all the commotion," Laura said. "Sam's been having more and more meetings over here the past few days. He's in the dining room." Laura walked Carl to the dining room. Sam was sitting at the wooden dining room table with Jessica, the Human Resources Director for the City of Neal.

"Hi Sam," Carl said entering the dining room. "Oh, hi Jessica, I didn't expect to see you here today."

"Thanks for coming over," Sam said. "I invited Jessica to be part of this meeting as we have something important to talk about."

Carl sat at the table across from Sam and Jessica. "Is it about the make-up of the interview panel for the new Accountant position? I just talked with Tom and assured him . . ."

Sam put his hand up. "No Carl this doesn't involve the Accountant position."

"Then what does it involve?" Carl asked.

"You," Jessica said.

"Me?"

"Yes you," Sam said. "There have been a few puzzling events that we wanted to talk to you about."

"What are they?" Carl asked.

"The first is your supervision of Karen Spencer and the DMAIC project. I talked with Karen and she gave me a much different account of their progress than you did."

"They have been making *some* progress," Carl said. "The team seems to go in stops and starts. But I've kept in touch with Karen just like you asked me."

"That's the issue," Sam said, "Karen mentioned that she's been giving you written reports about their progress."

"Yes she has," Carl said.

"Then how come the last time we talked," Sam said, "you stated that the effort was going nowhere. You suggested that I not bring up this topic during my performance review."

"That was my opinion," Carl said. "Maybe things have come together for the team since then."

"According to Karen," Sam said, "the DMAIC team was making great progress well before we talked."

"I don't know what to say," Carl said. "Maybe I just misinterpreted what Karen was reporting. I'm human you know and we all make mistakes."

"Understood," Jessica said. "But there is another and more pressing issue that we need to speak about."

"What's that?" Carl asked.

"It concerns the newspaper story," Jessica said, "that came out a few weeks ago."

"I told you," Carl said, "I left messages for the reporter to give him our side of the story, but he never returned my calls."

"It seems like you already *had been* in conversation with the reporter," Sam said.

"What?" Carl said.

"Carl, when I re-read that story," Sam said, "I realized that there was information reported that no one knew except for the City Manager's office. The Council Members were not aware of some of the details reported. I became suspicious and asked Robert in IT to check our e-mail history. It turns out that there were e-mails to this reporter several weeks before the story broke. The contents of the e-mails were deleted by the sender but we know that they were sent. And by looking at the back-up logs we traced the e-mails to your office."

"Sam, what are you accusing me of?" Carl said quietly.

"That's up to you," Sam said.

Carl was silent.

"Carl," Jessica said, "you can come clean with us today in this private setting. Or we can continue the investigation out in the public view. The choice is yours."

Carl stared off into the distance. His jaw trembled and he took a few deep breaths.

"OK, let's talk," Carl said.

"Can you give us an explanation?" Sam asked.

Carl was silent. He lowered his head. "Sam I never wanted to hurt you. I have great respect for you. You know that being in a leadership role in government is difficult. People watch everything that we do. Now with social media, sometimes the public hears about events before we do. We're on-call 24/7."

Sam and Jessica remained silent.

"I wanted to make a difference and help the City of Neal," Carl said. "But I didn't always agree with how the city was run. Sam again, I have great respect for you, but I just didn't agree with many of the decisions you made. It seems like my career ambitions got the best of me."

"What career ambitions?" Jessica asked.

Lowering his head, Carl said, "I wanted to be the City Manager."

No one spoke.

"When I saw how the City Council felt about Sam," Carl said, "I thought that this was my chance."

"We all have career goals," Sam said. "But what you did crossed ethical boundaries. It seems like you were trying to discredit me for my upcoming performance review. And shall I assume that if my contract wasn't renewed by the Council, then you'd have applied for my job?"

Carl nodded in agreement. "Sam I never wanted to hurt you. You have Laura and I figured that if your contract wasn't renewed that you would retire and everything would be fine. I'm a bachelor and my kids are all grown and living around the country. I guess I saw this opportunity to be City Manager as my last hurrah."

"I understand," Sam said. "But we do have to live by a code of ethics."

Carl nodded.

"Carl, this is a difficult situation," Jessica said. "But here is what I recommend. I suggest that you resign effective immediately . . . and take early retirement."

"I would publically state," Sam said, "that you retired due to personal issues. The details would be kept private."

"Carl," Jessica said, "if you agree with this, I'll call the office and have someone from Human Resources meet you at your office. They can help you pack up your personal belongings and we'll keep things very low key."

"What about my retirement and benefits?" Carl asked.

"We'll work with you on that," Jessica said. "You have plenty of years of service in the public sector and we'll work with you to ensure you take advantage of all of the benefits you've earned."

"Sam, what do you think?" Carl asked.

"I think it is the best course of action," Sam said.

Carl was silent. "Alright, make the call. I'll go clean out my office." Carl got up and left Sam and Laura's house.

Chapter 29

Two weeks passed. The elevator doors opened on the second floor of the Neal City Hall. Sam stepped out of the elevator and saw about ten city employees and a "Welcome Back" banner in big bold shiny letters. Yellow, red, and blue balloons were taped everywhere with black and white paper streamers hung on the wall.

"Whoa, what's this?" Sam asked.

"It's your official welcome back," Patty said.

"Glad you're back," Destin said.

"We missed you," David said.

"How are you feeling?" Tina asked.

"Good," Sam said. "And I'm certainly glad you didn't scream 'Welcome!!!' when the elevators opened. Otherwise, I may have had another heart attack!"

The group laughed.

"We're here to take good care of you Sam," Patty said. "Anything you need, just let us know."

Sam smiled. "Boy, I could get used to this. I should have had a heart attack years ago."

"Hush," Patty said. "I talked with Laura and she said that you can stay at work for four hours a day at most for now."

"Thank you everyone," Sam said. "I certainly appreciate this. And I must admit, that I missed you all."

"We're glad you're back," Tina said.

"Since I'm only here for half a day, please let me get into my office. I've been keeping up with my e-mail while I was at home, but I'm sure there's a pile of papers on my desk. So, thanks again everyone."

Some of the welcome committee shook Sam's hand or lightly patted him on the back. When everyone left, Sam went into his office.

It was bittersweet for Sam to be back in his office. He saw the piles of paperwork sitting on his desk. Some required his signature, others were for his review. He was relieved to be back, but his performance review was only days away. Sam pulled out a pad of writing paper and started jotting down accomplishments that he could bring up during the review. Later Sam printed some budget files from the computer to show that he has been fiscally conservative.

Patty knocked on the door. "Sam, Karen is here to see you."

"Send her in," Sam said.

Karen walked into Sam's office sat at a chair in front of his desk. "How are you feeling Sam?"

"Really glad to be back in my office," Sam said. "I certainly do better when I'm busy. I just hate sitting around all day."

"I know what you mean," Karen said.

"But I must admit," Sam said, "that I'm a bit nervous about my performance review. Over my career, I've been through many of these, but this one isn't sitting right with me."

"Can I tell you some good news about the pilot program for Development Services?" Karen said.

"I was hoping to hear some good news," Sam said. "That's why I called this meeting. What do you have for me?"

"We ran the pilot program for ten business days," Karen said, "and found that we were able to get 80% of the home renovation permits out within those ten days."

"Wow," Sam said. "That's even better that the goal of fifteen days."

"It is," Karen said. "And during those same two weeks, we also ran applications through the old process flow. And guess what—*not one* of them made it through during this time. They are all still somewhere in the queue waiting for a final determination."

"That's good to hear," Sam said.

"During those two weeks," Karen said, "we only received two commercial applications and one custom home permit. We're still working on these, but our turnaround goal is longer for these complicated permits."

"So 80% of the home renovation permits that went through the new process flow made it out within ten days?" Sam asked.

"Yes," Karen said. "Now these are still preliminary numbers, but the new process flow seems to be working. And we did find a few things to tweak in the process during this pilot program."

"What's that?" Sam asked.

"Previously," Karen said, "*all* permits were going to the Environmental Health department. The Health technician realized that home renovation permits don't need a health review and she talked with Keisha and her supervisor Erika. They agreed that only new home construction and commercial permits needed to be routed for Health's approval. It's a small change, but it also cut some time out of the review cycle."

Sam grinned. "That's fantastic—when front line workers start making suggestions on how to improve things, then I know we've made an impact."

"I plan to keep running this pilot test for a bit longer," Karen said. "The longer we run it, the more we can tweak the process before we do a final implementation."

"Your results are very timely," Sam said. "My review is later this week and I'll definitely mention this."

"I'm glad," Karen said. "I think that you'll do just fine."

Sam stood and shook Karen's hand. "Thanks again, Karen."

"It was my pleasure."

Chapter 30

The following week, Karen entered the DMAIC conference room. The group was already together. "Today," Karen said, "we'll wrap up our DMAIC project."

"How sad," Cindy said.

"I agree," Brad said. "You know, after meeting together for a period of weeks, we've really jelled as a team. Tim, Keisha, Karen, Patel, Cindy, Adam thank you for being a part of this effort."

"We've formed a unique bond," Keisha said. "By supporting each other, being creative, and working toward a common goal, we've accomplished a lot. And we owe a huge thank you to Karen for being our facilitator."

"You guys and gals have been great to work with," Karen said. "I'm proud of the work we've done here and also sad to see our weekly ritual coming to an end."

Tim and Patel nodded.

"But we're not finished yet," Karen said. "Today we'll work on the Control phase of DMAIC, and there are four things we need to accomplish. First we have to establish a monitoring plan to ensure that the new process continues to meet the goals we set. Next, we need to develop a response plan if the new process is not meeting those goals. And finally, we need to document our efforts so that others will understand what we accomplished and also learn from it."

"But you only listed three items," Patel said. "I thought that you said we had four things to accomplish today."

"I was holding the last one for a surprise," Karen said. "When we are finished today, we celebrate. I ordered a cake and sodas and we'll have our own party."

"I like that last part," Tim said.

"OK, then let's get going," Adam said. "To heck with my diet, I'm looking forward to some cake."

"Let's start with the monitoring plan," Karen said. "Since the pilot program is giving us the results we wanted, we'll make it the new permanent process over the next several weeks. The preliminary results are good and we need to make sure that we continually monitor the time that it takes to issue a permit."

"We have a feature on our existing software," Brad said, "that we haven't used in the past. It's a 'dashboard display' and it can give us real time feedback on how long it takes a permit to travel through the system."

"Tell us more," Karen said.

"Since we are now e-mailing files," Brad said, "the software can track when a permit application was put into the system and also track when it was reviewed and returned by each of the five divisions. I can code the application as being a house renovation, a new home construction, or a commercial permit."

"And what were those deadlines again?" Karen said.

"We set fifteen days for home renovation permits," Tim said. "Twenty days for new home construction, and twenty-five days for commercial applications."

"Good," Karen said. "So Brad, when you set up the dashboard, please separate out the three different types of permits and monitor the different due dates. And you can share that information with Larry, the department director, so you can keep a close eye on the new process."

"Is there anything else that we should be monitoring?" Patel asked.

"That's a good start," Karen said. "You always want to keep things simple. And this leads us into our second goal for today, which is to establish a 'response plan'."

"Can you tell us more about a response plan?" Tim asked.

"A response plan," Karen said, "is a written set of procedures that should be followed if the permits are not being issued in the stated time. If Brad and Larry review the 'dashboard', and they notice that the home renovation permits are taking longer than fifteen days to issue, their response plan is a set of actions to investigate and correct the problem."

"That makes sense," Tim said.

"If we are not meeting our goal," Brad said, "the first place I'd look is if one or more of the divisions are late in getting their responses back to me."

"Can the 'dashboard' software track this?" Cindy asked.

"I think it can," Brad said. "Since the software can track when an application was e-mailed to each division, we can also track when that application was e-mailed back to me. I can then look if one or more of the divisions have been late in getting me their response."

"OK," Karen said. "Let's assume that Brad finds that, for example, the Safety division is falling behind, what should be our response?"

"Since I'm in Safety, let me handle this one," Adam said. "The first thing that I would do would be to look at how long it was taking to issue the permits. Then I would look at our staffing for the previous week. Were some of the technicians out sick or on vacation that week? If so, then the problem should be resolved when they return. If not, then I would look at the number of permits we reviewed that week. Maybe we had a surge in the numbers and should consider hiring a temp to help us out. And finally, I would also look at the types of permits we were reviewing over that past week. Maybe we had a few big commercial permits that slowed us down."

"That's a good action plan," Karen said. "If your division is not meeting the stated goal, then you can do a mini DMAIC review. And just like Adam outlined, you can quickly define the problem, measure it, analyze it, improve it, and then set controls in place."

"Since we now know DMAIC," Keisha said, "we should be able to run that mini DMAIC project in just a few hours."

"Yes," Karen said. "Don't get too elaborate. Just look why you're not meeting your goal and then take corrective action. My assignment for everyone here today is: when you get back to your office, write out your response plan. Be sure to include who is responsible to taking each action. If you are prepared with a response plan, the resolution to the problem will come a lot quicker."

"Sound good," Patel said. "It's good to be prepared."

"Our next task," Karen said, "is to document what we have accomplished through our DMAIC project."

"Why's this necessary?" Cindy asked.

"Communication and standardization," Karen said. "The first is to communicate to others how the DMAIC process works and what we have accomplished. You can do this relatively simply through a story board."

"We did one of those," Tim said, "when we completed the mail delivery process analysis when I worked for Angola County."

"Can you tell the group about it?" Karen asked.

"Sure," Tim said. "Our project facilitator mentioned that even though we have e-mail and company newsletters, these aren't always the best methods to communicate with your fellow employees."

"I agree," Patel said. "I get so many messages in my e-mail, I don't always have time to read them all. I look for messages that require my immediate action and I generally delete those that are just information."

"That's the double edged sword of e-mail," Tim said. "It's easy to send e-mails and just as easy for the receiver to delete them. So when I was employed at the county, we presented our DMAIC findings over a series of face-to-face department meetings. And to help us in our presentation, we made a story board out of that same poster board that our kids use at school."

"You mean that white foam board," Cindy said, "that you buy in an art supply store?"

"Yep," Tim said. "We used the tri-fold board so that you could easily stand it up on a table when you were presenting at a meeting."

"What did you put on the board?" Brad asked.

"We divided each of the three panels in half," Tim said. "So we end up with six sections. On the first section we gave an overview of the project and the results we obtained. But we used lots of visuals, such as charts and graphs, and a minimal amount of words. Then we devoted each of the five remaining sections to the five parts of DMAIC."

"So one section was devoted to Define," Adam said, "and the others were devoted to Measure, Analyze, Improve, and Control?"

"That's right," Tim said. "And each of these five sections had lots of visuals, such as the before and after flow charts, and a minimum amount of words. When we presented our finding at the department meetings, it was easy to just look at the poster board and tell the audience what we did. And I was surprised at the end of the meeting, how many people came up and looked at the poster board. It was something they could quickly view in about thirty seconds and they had a complete picture of what we did."

"Thanks Tim," Karen said. "These face-to-face meetings are so import-ant to teach Lean and Six Sigma to others by showing them the progress other departments have made. I've found that once they see the results, other departments want to run a DMAIC project as well."

"Also," Tim said, "in between department meetings, we left the poster board standing up on a table in the cafeteria. Lots of people stopped to look at it as it was colorful and easy to understand."

"Thank again Tim," Karen said. "I mentioned previously that the second reason to document our DMAIC work is standardization."

"Tell us more about that," Keisha said.

"In order to continuously improve," Karen said, "it's necessary for everyone doing the same task to standardize on their work process. You don't want one health technician reviewing the application one way and another health technician reviewing it in another way."

"That been a continual problem for us," Brad said. "In the past, we've had techs from the same department giving conflicting information to the customer. This really slows things down and frustrates the customer."

"The more you can standardize the process that each division uses," Karen said, "and the interpretation of the codes, the better you will be. Standardization also helps with cross training employees. So if one person is out sick, another person can do his or her task with the minimum of disruption to the process."

"Standardization is something that I plan on doing," Brad said. "I've wanted to it for a while and now's my opportunity. I plan to write out a detailed set of procedures for each technician to follow. And I'll address the issue of conflicting information so that we stay consistent with our communication. I'm looking forward to it."

"Sounds great," Karen said. "OK, who's ready for some cake?"

"I am," Patel said.

"Me too," Tim said.

Karen stepped out of the room and returned with a cart containing a chocolate cake and drinks. The cake was frosted with: "Congratulations to the DMAIC team for a job well done."

"Karen, as our facilitator," Keisha said, "we would like you to cut the cake."

"Sure," Karen said. "It would be my honor."

"Karen," Adam said, "since I'm on a diet, only give me a half slice."

"Yeah right," Patel said, "we know that you'll be back for the other half and then seconds and thirds."

Karen cut the cake and started passing out the slices, forks, and napkins to the group.

"I'm real excited to make this the new permanent process at Development Services," Brad said. "I talked with some of the employees that were involved with the pilot run and they were very thankful for the change."

"I noticed that too," Keisha said. "I'm already starting to think of ways to use DMAIC on some of the Environmental Health processes we use every day."

"The other day I was having lunch with Ryan in Utilities," Tim said. "He heard about the progress we made and wanted me to make a presentation to his staff."

"This is a powerful new way for looking at processes," Patel said. "I'm real excited to move forward."

As they were enjoying the cake and drinks, Sam's assistant Patty knocked on the conference room door.

"Karen, can I see you for a second?" Patty asked.

Karen stepped out into the hallway.

"Sam would like to see you right away," Patty said.

"Now?" Karen asked.

"Yes," Patty said, "Sam said as soon as possible."

Karen was concerned about the tone in Patty's voice. She went back into the conference room and politely excused herself from the party.

Chapter 31

Karen sat outside of Sam's office. As she waited for him, she remembered how she had felt the first time she met him several months earlier. But this time she was worried about the results of Sam's performance review and his future with the City of Neal.

"Hi Karen," Sam said. "Come into my office."

Karen entered and sat at the oval table. She hoped that she didn't look as worried as she felt. Sam closed his office door and sat across from her.

"Karen, I have good news and bad news," Sam said. "The good news is that I *conditionally* passed my performance review. The Mayor and Council agreed to extend my contract for one year."

Karen breathed a sigh of relief. "That's great to hear. What's the bad news?"

"I will have another performance review in twelve months," Sam said. "The Council gave me a list of things to accomplish between now and then. They were very stern stating that I needed to complete this new list of tasks within the year, or my contract will not be extended."

"But I'm glad that you still have a job," Karen said.

"Me too," Sam said. "It turns out that the new City Council members didn't completely align themselves behind Trisha. Even Mayor Denim was very supportive of the work we've been doing."

"Did the DMAIC review at Development Services come up?" Karen asked.

Sam smiled. "It sure did, and I owe you a great big thank you."

Karen smiled.

"The Council was closely watching our efforts there," Sam said. "Although a bit irregular, they did interview several home owners who submitted an application under the new system."

"And the comments?" Karen asked.

"All were very positive," Sam said. "They liked that we combined the three applications into one, they liked having one point of contact to deal with for questions, and they *really liked*, that we gave them an answer in about two weeks time."

"I am so glad to hear that," Karen said.

"Karen, I must admit," Sam said, "when we first talked about DMAIC I had my doubts. I wasn't sure if it would work for government and if the city employees would accept the change. To my surprise the DMAIC review significantly cut the time to respond to the applicant. And the employees that use the new process actually love it. They enjoy that we took the obstacles away from them so they could do their jobs. You really streamlined the process."

"After using DMAIC for years," Karen said, "I knew that we would get positive results. Sam I want to thank you for giving me this opportunity."

"It was a leap of faith," Sam said. "But sometimes when our back is up against the wall, we need to get rid of the thinking that got us into the problem in the first place."

"Nice thought," Karen said.

"The other thing that surprised me about DMAIC and process improvement," Sam said, "is that I've been doing this for years, but didn't realize it."

Karen raised an eyebrow.

"As you know," Sam said, "my passion is renovating old houses and over time I've renovated probably half a dozen of them. And when I think back, I was doing DMAIC and process improvement when I was renovating old homes."

"What do you mean?" Karen asked.

"I realized that both homes and processes start out neat and efficient. Over time a house degrades from wear and tear. I'm sure that when it was built, it served the family that lived in it just fine. Over time, their needs changed and things just wore out. But, when we live in our homes most of us just accept this and continue living there. It is only when a new person buys the house, like me, and I look at it through a different set of eyes that I see what needs to be changed. When I bought this current property, I realized that the windows had to be replaced, the kitchen needed a make-over, and the master bedroom closet needed more room."

Karen waited for Sam to say more.

"And our processes at work, such as at Development Services, also need to be looked at through a new set of eyes," Sam said. "Over time, processes degrade due to changes in technology or customer needs. But too often, we continue with the old process, just like a family accepts their house getting old. But when you look at a process through a new set of eyes, like I was doing with the houses I purchased to fix up, the problems were obvious."

"Sam, that's a great analogy," Karen said.

"I owe a lot to you," Sam said. "I mentioned earlier, that the Council gave a list of items to complete in this next year. And at the top of the list was to incorporate Lean and Six Sigma throughout *all processes* at the city. And that's where you come in Karen."

"Me?"

"Yes, I need your help to teach and spread Lean and Six Sigma. I want the City of Neal to be progressive and a model of efficiency."

"How am I involved?"

"Karen, I would like to offer you the position of Lean and Six Sigma Deployment Director for the City of Neal."

Karen's eyes opened wide.

"You would report directly to me and you would have my support and authority. Your mission would be to bring Lean and Six Sigma to all of the departments in the City of Neal. What do you think?"

Karen was silent for a moment and stared off in the distance. She turned to Sam and said, "Yes, I accept this position and I'm up for the challenge."

Sam smiled. "Terrific."

"So we only have a year?" Karen asked.

"Yep," Sam said.

"OK, that's not much time, so here are some of my thoughts on how to roll out Lean and Six Sigma. We'll start with the Department of . . ."

* * *

End

Index

Share Your Success Stories

I would love to hear about your Lean and Six Sigma success stories.

Tell me what the problem was, how you solved it, and the end result. With your permission, I will publish these stories to demonstrate the power of process improvement to make government more efficient.

Please send any success stories or questions to Success@StreamlineGovt.com.

Thank you.

Richard Baron
Lean Six Sigma Black Belt
Process & Project Coordinator
Coconino County, Arizona
Richard@StreamlineGovt.com
www.StreamlineGovt.com

About the Author

Richard Baron is a Process & Project Coordinator for Coconino County in Arizona. There he leads the process improvement efforts for the county, and started the Lean Government committee. Previously, he was a consultant for the Arizona Manufacturing Extension Partnership (MEP), a nationwide organization providing Lean consultation to manufacturers. He has been involved with manufacturing for most of his career.

Richard is an active member of the Alliance for Innovation (www.transform gov.org), Arizona City/County Management Association (ACMA) (www. azmanagement.org), International City/County Management Association (ICMA) (www.icma.org), Arizona Association of Counties (AACO) (www.azcounties. org), National Association of Counties (NACO) (www.naco.org), and National Association of County Administrators (NACA) (www.countyadministrators.org).

He has produced and recorded seminars on Lean and Six Sigma, which are available through the Alliance for Innovation at www.transformgov.org.

He holds a Lean Six Sigma Black Belt from Acuity Institute, a Bachelor of Science in Industrial Engineering from Arizona State University, a Master's in International Management from Thunderbird School of Global Management, and a Master's in Business Administration from Arizona State University.

Order Print or E-book Copies of *Streamline*

Streamline can be purchased in print version at www.CreateSpace.com (an Amazon company).

Streamline is also available in print and as an e-book at www.Amazon.com.

For a volume discount on orders of 10 or more copies of the book, please send a request to Sales@StreamlineGovt.com.

CPSIA information can be obtained
at www.ICGtesting.com
Printed in the USA
LVHW01s0000260817
546432LV00004B/120/P